Praise for
When She Comes Back

"Artfully written, *When She Comes Back* is the powerful account of Ronit Plank's childhood, from her earliest years of communal living within an Israeli kibbutz, to the tumultuous years in NYC while her absent mother followed Bhagwan Shree Rajneesh, the guru and now infamous sex-cult leader from the Netflix documentary *Wild Wild Country*. In this fascinating coming-of-age memoir, Ronit Plank poignantly explores the resilience of a child longing for her mother and ultimately leads us along her path to reconciliation. *When She Comes Back* is a stunning debut."
– Jason Allen, Author of *The East End*

"*When She Comes Back* tells the almost unbelievable story of a girl left behind by a mother who fell into the thrall of one of the most infamous cult leaders of the 20th century, following the Bhagwan Shri Rajneesh to India, then the doomed Oregon featured in the documentary "Wild, Wild Country," while her two young children grew up in the company of various relatives and a father who wasn't finished growing up himself. Despite the extraordinary circumstances of her childhood, Plank's story will feel relatable to anyone who has ever wondered if their family is "normal," or experienced the more routine childhood trauma of divorce. Empathetic, richly detailed, and self-aware, *When She Comes Back* is a heartbreaking, hopeful story about loss, resilience, and growing up too soon."
– Erica C. Barnett, Author of *Quitter*

"A beautifully written and wrenching story of abandonment and resilience, *When She Comes Back* grabbed me by the heart. I could not put this powerful memoir down."
– Aspen Matis, bestselling author of *Your Blue Is Not My Blue* and *Girl in the Woods*

WHEN SHE COMES BACK

a memoir

Ronit Plank

Motina Books
Van Alstyne, Texas

Some names have been changed to protect individuals' privacy.

Published by Motina Books, LLC, Van Alstyne, Texas
www.MotinaBooks.com

Library of Congress Cataloguing-in-Publication Data

Names: Plank, Ronit
Title: When She Comes Back/Ronit Plank
Description: First Edition. | Van Alstyne: Motina Books, 2021
Identifiers: LCCN: 2021931125 | ISBN-13: 978-1-945060-26-7 (hardcover) | ISBN-13: 978-1-945060-18-2 (ebook) | ISBN-13: 978-1-945060-19-9 (paperback)
Subjects: BISAC: BIOGRAPHY & AUTOBIOGRAPHY/Women | BIOGRAPHY & AUTOBIOGRAPHY/Religious | BIOGRAPHY & AUTOBIOGRAPHY/Cultural, Ethnic & Regional/General

Cover Design: Jon Gray, gray318
Interior Design: Diane Windsor

For my family, especially my husband and my children
and
For my sister, who lit the way.

.

A soul in belief is a delicate thing—it can be exploited or liberated, depending on circumstances.

    -Mallika Rao "Why I Hate Gurus", *Vulture*

Prologue, Newark, 1978

When my mother told us she was going to visit Bhagwan Shree Rajneesh's ashram, I was six years old and my sister was three. She was taking us to see our father for the first time since he'd left the year before but I remember the promise she made: she would be back at the end of the summer to collect Nava and me and bring us home to Seattle. I had no idea at the time that she would be absent from my life for decades to come—or that my mother was committing herself to a cult.

It was well past my bedtime when we landed at Newark Airport. I pressed my face to the window as the plane taxied and came to a stop but could only make out a few small luggage trucks pulling up to meet us in the dark.

"Come on, Ronit," she said, grabbing her purse and hoisting Nava into her arms. I glanced at the adults standing in the aisle behind me and followed my mother off the plane. The sticky June air hit me as soon as I stepped on the jetway and though it was late the terminal teemed with people. I kept my eyes on my mother who walked ahead with Nava in her arms, searching for my father, her mouth tight, her face unreadable.

I, too, searched for my father among the men near the gate, though I wasn't sure I remembered exactly what he looked like and I wonder now if he felt the same. We hadn't seen each other since he'd come to our rental house after their divorce a year before to say goodbye. My mother slowed to a stop and put Nava down. My father stood just ahead, mustached and big-haired, wearing the same thick glasses he'd had for years, and a long-sleeved, collared shirt. I leaned down and told my sister, "That's Daddy."

I smiled at him like I might at a stranger, unsure if he would smile back, and suddenly, before I had time to see what his response would be, he picked me up and hugged me, swinging me around as he did. It was a change from the tentativeness between my mother and me. There had been less of her to hold onto for a while.

I focused on the geometric patterns on his shirt, the pack of Winston Lights in the pocket, his familiar smell. Before I was ready for him to let me go, he put me down and picked up my sister.

My parents stood facing each other, together in a way they hadn't been in so long, but I didn't feel any surge of relief, saw no sign they loved each other again. So, I smiled because I knew I should feel happy, though I didn't. I thought maybe my mother would feel better when she saw my father, but something was wrong.

People in the airport moved in all directions, I heard unfamiliar languages and accents, smelled leather and perfume and hairspray. The excitement of travel pulsed and swelled all around us, but I homed in on the silence swirling between my parents directly above me. I had been sucked into their whirlpool, once again drawn to their center.

My father tried to make eye contact with my mother but she kept looking away. His jaw clenched. She adjusted her purse strap, flicked her hair away from her eyes.

I didn't have the details, and at age six couldn't have truly understood even if I had, but I felt the dissonance: two people who had given me life no longer wanted anything to do with each other. Yet there I was, a reminder of their connection, and of their mistakes. Someone they had no choice but to take care of.

My mother bent down toward me. "I have to catch my plane."

I wasn't ready for her to go. I wanted someone to tell me again what was next, but instead she gave me a hug. I hugged her back but didn't mean to be saying goodbye. She kissed Nava, still in my father's arms. I tried to catch my breath but hiccupped air.

If I had known then what was to come, would I have run after her and told her to stay?

My father stood next to me, my sister in his arms. My mother walked away from us, toward her gate, her frame shrinking in the bustling airport crowd, smaller and smaller until I couldn't see her anymore.

The Past Comes Calling

When I was grown and had two children, friends who knew my family's story began to message me about a six-part documentary on Bhagwan Shree Rajneesh called *Wild Wild Country*. The series looked good, they told me; I might find it interesting. But I hesitated. When I was a teenager, I had promised myself that I would try not to expose myself to Bhagwan ever again. I didn't want to see his face, hear his droning voice, or know anything more about the men and women who, like my mother, gave up their loved ones to follow him. He wasn't a man to me, or even just a guru. He was a time and a place, a natural disaster; a force that had wrecked my family. I blamed him for taking my mother away.

But the idea of being able to see where my mother had gone and what she had done when she left me and my sister Nava hounded me. The story of Bhagwan and his ashrams was like a distant, mythical tale from long ago that I had been able to only partially piece together from memories and scattered conversations. Now Bhagwan Shree Rajneesh and his ashrams were resurfacing, brought to life again with hours of never-seen-before interviews and footage, and with them the question I didn't realize I've wanted the answer for since the first time she left: Was what Bhagwan gave her worth leaving Nava and me for?

On a chilly night during the spring *Wild Wild Country* aired I pulled a purple sleeping bag off the back of a chair where it was unzipped and airing out from one of my kids' recent overnights. I gathered it up around me, moving the cold teeth of the zipper away from my chin. My husband pressed start on episode one and, with my arms crossed tightly against my chest and my body as still as I could make it, I braced myself.

~

When I think of Bhagwan Shree Rajneesh, I see my mother in sunset-colored clothing and a black-beaded necklace around her neck, a mala with a photo of Bhagwan's face dangling from the end. This was what all of his sannyasins or followers wore. Now forty years later, thousands of them appeared in frame after frame of the documentary: sannyasins dancing, sannyasins laughing, sannyasins doing ashram chores, sannyasins meditating in a massive pavilion, and hundreds of them lined up along a one-lane road waiting for the moment when Bhagwan would drive by in one of his ninety-six Rolls Royces, hoping for a glimpse of their master.

I had first seen men and women draped in orange clothing at the meetings my mother took us to a year before she left Nava and me with our father at Newark Airport.

What struck me when we went to these meditations was the adults' unusual behavior towards children. They didn't make more than hazy eye contact with us; there wasn't any sense of curiosity that two little ones had arrived, the only kids in the place. No impulse at all to settle us in or help make us feel welcome. Even though people in Seattle seemed pretty reserved—make that really reserved—grownups usually tried to be friendly toward us. The way these men and women looked around us, through us, troubled me. I couldn't verbalize my worry then, but it nagged at me that my mother didn't seem to notice that the people she wanted to spend more time with basically ignored her children.

I was already becoming more insecure in my attachment to her but I still knew from my first four years of life on a kibbutz in Israel that grown-ups were supposed to guide children and treat them with

5

gentleness. I would later learn that Bhagwan felt children were a distraction, that they made spiritual growth difficult to attain. In fact, he encouraged sterilization and vasectomies for sannyasins on his ashram, and later on his ranch in Antelope, Oregon. Decades later my mother told me herself that "Bhagwan taught that children were obstacles to enlightenment."

Bhagwan had been a student of philosophy in India and introduced what he coined "Dynamic Meditation" back in 1970. That was also the year he initiated his first group of sannyasins for his ashram in Pune. He handpicked new names for the men and women who joined him and they donned the orange of Hindu holy men and the mala with their master's face. But what set Bhagwan apart from other gurus in India was that he encouraged his sannyasins to embrace a celebratory lifestyle rather than an austere or abstinent one. He lectured in both English and Hindi and espoused sex as the first step to "super-consciousness." By 1974 he had a six-acre ashram in Pune where Westerners flocked to in order to live and work and learn. They took part in therapy groups where, in the early days of the ashram, sex and violence were documented to have been used to help followers reach "breakthroughs" on their paths to awareness.

By 1977, Bhagwan's teachings were gaining momentum in the Western world. He had published multiple books and had his very own Rajneeshee Center in our Capital Hill neighborhood in Seattle. My mother was on food stamps with no family living nearby, and no close network to help her with Nava and me, now that my father had left for New Jersey, so she started bringing us to events at the Rajneeshee Center and different Seattle-area homes. At the first one she took us to she settled us on a sofa and found a spot for herself on the floor in the hushed and candlelit room.

Perched on my knees to see better I surveyed the sannyasins and soon-to-be-sannnyasins from my cushion, how they sat motionless and slack-jawed for almost an hour while Bhagwan's slow, languorous voice oozed from the speaker on the wall. I'd left Israel a year and a half before and was still new to English but I caught the unusual way he lingered on certain syllables, how he drew out the "s" at the end of his words like a tired snake. It was as if he had all the time in the world to say whatever it was he was saying. The tape seemed to last forever, and though at three different times I was certain he was finished making his point, he started up again. Nava had fallen asleep next to me so she wasn't able to distract me and I didn't think I could take any more.

I wanted to levitate up off the sofa, up past the listless sea of heads around me to another place where I wasn't trapped listening to this monotonous voice, where I didn't have to go to a stranger's house at night and be near adults who didn't care anything about me. I knew that if my father still lived in Seattle, he would have made sure that I never had to attend one of these gatherings again. I stared at my mother's face in the candlelight, willing her to open her eyes, to feel me trying to connect with her so she'd realize that it was time to leave. It was almost like she'd forgotten I was there, forgotten I was supposed to be home getting ready for bed. I wanted to tiptoe over to her and whisper that this had gone on too long but I didn't want to get into trouble. I was reliable and compliant, I would never have cried or drawn negative attention to myself; I did what my mother expected me to. Plus, and most importantly, she had promised me there would be cookies at the end of the meeting if I behaved and that's the real reason I cooperated. She knew I was a pushover for food. Even as a toddler in Israel, wherever we went I wanted to know if there would be treats. I wish now I had been more of a pain in the neck and much less bribable—maybe then she wouldn't have lugged us around to so many meetings.

Finally, the tape ended and I watched the adults embrace each other. The lights came on and my mother drifted back over to collect us. The cookies they served were dry and store-bought, nothing special, definitely not worth sitting through a meditation for. I was sure I wouldn't fall for a bribe like that again. But I did.

When the Rajneeshee Center held a party one Sunday afternoon, I cashed in as soon as we arrived and took my Graham cracker outside to eat. Part of the backyard was shaded, the ground damp and packed like it is much of the time in Seattle. Other parts were thick and grassy and lit up in startling sunlight. The lawn and the people strewn around it were so bright in places, they appeared almost bleached out.

Sannyasins were lying around the grass with languid smiles, some massaging each other. Their eyes stopped just short of focusing on their surroundings; I couldn't tell if they were actually seeing anything they looked at. Aside from Nava, who was with my mother somewhere inside, there were no other children around, so I sat near a woman my mother had introduced me to at another meeting and ate my Graham cracker. After a little while, she reached over for my foot and asked me if I'd like a little massage. I'd never had a massage before but nodded okay because that was easier than telling her, "no thanks." She rolled her thumbs over the ball of my right foot and pressed in, working her way to my arch which felt good but also a little strange.

After enough moments had passed so as not to be rude, I asked, "Do *you* want a massage?" and I moved my foot away. I wasn't completely at ease with her handling my body, really for anybody here to handle my body, but offering to do something for her rather than accept something from her felt safer to me. I had a feeling it was a better way to control the situation. No way I was going to touch her feet though, so I stood behind her and placed my hands on her shoulders and squeezed, the way I saw some of the other adults were doing. I worked my thumbs into her back, kneading with my fingers, trying to replicate what she had done when she massaged me.

"You have strong hands," she said.

From over her shoulder I checked her face and she was smiling, so I kept massaging her but with even more enthusiasm. I've always been such a sucker for compliments.

I do think I knew this wasn't an ordinary or normal situation. I didn't love being there with her instead of my mother, but I appreciated that this woman had recognized me for being good at something. I had value even if it was only because of the power in my hands.

I don't know if hypervigilant kids are made or born, if I would have picked up on everything that was going on around me anyway, or if I became insecure and watchful because I didn't feel my mother watching over me. I don't know what it's like to be free enough as a kid to try anything or wander anywhere because you know your mother is keeping you in mind, that no matter what, you'll be safe because she's focused on you.

Part of me sees my mother as strong, tall, busy, with an aura around her I couldn't approach. A combination of contemplation, worry, and a desire to be somewhere better; the side of her that would ultimately push her to find what she was looking for. The other part of me sees the sad, lost side of her, which in many ways was maybe as young and inexperienced as I was. When she and my father left Israel after eight years on the kibbutz, she didn't even know how to write a check—now she was a single mother alone in a new city, searching and unsure of how to proceed, about to collapse with the impossibility of being on her own.

I see somebody who was never properly mothered herself, who wasn't able to give all of herself, now being forced to drain every last ounce. She was fighting for control of her life, for direction and meaning, as if she were locked in a brutal tug-of-war. The difficulty was, my sister and I were on the other end of the rope. I had no idea that afternoon on the lawn that I was months away from losing her.

The Great Escape

Not long ago I heard a fellow teacher at my synagogue describe the Negev desert to her students as a place where it was "hard to grow things and difficult to survive." I felt as if she were speaking to me. Our Negev desert kibbutz in Israel is where the seed of my family began and would try to grow, in the sandy soil beneath the glaring sun, half a world away from everything my parents had known. It was where I was born.

The very first time my father met my mother she was inside a silo stomping on silage. A meet-cute as unconventional as a lot of my family's history, my father climbed a ladder, saw my mother in high boots mucking around the fermenting crops, and cracked a joke. He was tall and skinny with dark-rimmed, thick glasses, and light-brown curly hair. He was smart and, as my mother tells it, knew how to talk to women. She flirted back.

It was 1967 in Hightstown, New Jersey. My mother was nineteen, my father twenty-one, and separately they had answered the same call. They were on a farm learning how to grow sorghum and wheat and care for livestock before boarding ships for Israel where they'd been matched to a kibbutz. Back then, before many of them became privatized, a kibbutz was a settlement—almost always secular—where people lived communally. Kibbutz members were both owners and management and did whatever the job was specific to that kibbutz, like factory work or farming. In return for manual labor and adhering to kibbutz rules, their adoptive community rewarded my parents with predictability and bona fide roles. Moving to Israel to cultivate land and new relationships was finding home; an antidote to family discord and abuse; an escape from their respective histories.

Neither of them had very nurturing childhoods. My father had moved around as a kid and his parents had divorced when he was in middle school. He had spent his college summers in Mississippi doing civil rights work and traveling, hitchhiking by himself across the country and back again a couple times, doing laboring jobs along the way and sleeping at the side of the road. He dropped out of college after two years and got a small apartment in Manhattan and a job with a publishing company, but soon went out to the farm in Hightstown while he tried to decide what to do with his life.

My mother's parents also divorced when she was in middle school. She was living in Manhattan and going to Hunter College when friends invited her to New Jersey to visit the farm. For her the place was a revelation. She'd never been part of any kind of social movement nor had she traveled beyond the Brooklyn neighborhood where she'd grown up. In Hightstown for the first time she was part of something that mattered, finally around people who appreciated her personality, her enthusiasm, and work ethic, in a place where she felt accepted.

My parents were young, Jewish, and wanting to belong to something or someone. When they weren't working with the crops and animals, they sought each other out. The days were long and they quickly fell in love. It must have been intoxicating for them to find themselves valued and depended on, to sink into bed at night with their bodies sore from operating heavy equipment and lifting bales of hay, their anxious, uncertain minds finally at rest. They were doing something nobody in their family had ever done, living in a way no one they knew had before. The regimen was perfect for my mother, who longed to have a meaningful role, and for my father who was sentimental at heart and envisioned himself taming the land and connecting with nature—creating something from nothing like a hero from the novel he wanted to write someday.

After they finished their training in New Jersey my parents shipped out to Israel, in August 1968. They spent their first ten months on Kibbutz Gal-On, a more established community with a suburban feel, and then requested a transfer to Kibbutz Lahav. They chose Lahav because it was a younger kibbutz and more rugged and untamed. Lahav was in the south of Israel near Be'er Sheva, in the Negev desert, which from a distance is rolling and rippled, beige and purple-tinted, shadowed and bright, not jagged looking and dry. Closer up it's a land where the Bedouin herded goats, where Ben Gurion University was established in 1969, and where I would return during college for a semester and hear an Israeli student describe it as "the armpit of Israel."

About two hundred people lived on the kibbutz. Some younger, unattached women and men passed through to volunteer for several months or a year, but most of the kibbutzniks were married couples with children. Each married couple had their own one-bedroom, one-bathroom bungalow with a kitchenette, but every other aspect of life was shared and decisions on the kibbutz were made as a group.

My father wanted to get married; my mother was unsure. He had proposed to her under a tree in Central Park the summer before they left for Israel with an engagement ring made from the diamond ring his grandfather had left him. I think he loved her and he wanted a family of his own, to create what he'd never had in his life—to be the father his was not. Whatever the reasons, theirs was not a love story of classic novels and romantic films, but more the *why-the-hell-not* variety. When two other couples on Kibbutz Lahav set a date for a double wedding in December of 1968, my father convinced my mother the time was right and they turned the double wedding into a triple. I think she worried that they weren't a good match, or maybe that she wasn't ready. I don't think it's easy to make a decision like that if you have no healthy example from your own family or life to follow.

My mother had grown up without affection or even people who

told her they loved her. Her father had been warm but once he and my grandmother divorced, he was soon out of the picture. My Grandma Lina seemed dissatisfied with my mother from the moment their relationship began and my mother never understood why. My grandma didn't give her the attention her troubled older brother Bobby got and couldn't seem to muster a trace of the affection or playfulness she showed my mother's younger sister Gloria. My mother grew up knowing something must have been wrong with her, because no matter what she did it wasn't enough, and she couldn't make her mother happy. Beliefs that, ironically, I too would have about myself by the time my childhood was over.

In pictures from their wedding day my mother and father beam. She removed her glasses for the occasion. The contrast of her light brown eyes and long dark hair swept up and away from her face with the fairness of her skin, and the whiteness of her mini-dress and veil is sharp, but there is softness to her. In one photo her veil radiates from around her head and spills from the car she steps out of, her pretty teeth revealed in her wide smile. You would never be able to tell she'd hesitated to marry my father. You would never know she wasn't sure she'd made the right decision.

I used to look at my parents' photo albums in elementary school and try to understand how, if my mother looked this happy in their wedding photos, she could have become so unhappy later. It scared me. It was a reminder of how she could change her mind, of why it wasn't smart to believe in people.

Sabra

My mother had me when she was twenty-four, after she and my father had been on Kibbutz Lahav for four years.

Before I understood or even had an inkling that people leave—even people who are supposed to take care of you, the kibbutz was my Eden. My father brought me out for walks on his shoulders and we visited the kibbutz horses, pigs, and turkeys in the farm area, and animals in the little kibbutz zoo. He taught me to lower my voice and to be gentle; to kneel on the ground and let them approach me so they felt comfortable. I got to pet geese and hold downy newborn goats, their velvet ears flopping around their dazed faces. He helped our dog, a beagle-German Shepard mix named after a comic strip character, Auggie Doggie, get used to me and trust me.

I walked the paved sunlit paths in any direction I chose—often by myself, because I was safe there alone—and every afternoon I joined my mother and father on the lawn in front of our home to sit with our friends and have cookies, fruit, and tea while a gentle breeze blew across the hillside, even in the summer. Afternoons on the lawn were my favorite time, near my mother who chatted happily with the other women while I played with my friends.

On the kibbutz in the old days, babies spent the first six weeks in their parents' flat and were then moved to the Beit Tinokot, the

Children's House. The kibbutz Children's House system was part of an early twentieth century model designed to enable women to be equal partners with men, to liberate them from having to stay home doing domestic chores while the men went out to war. Many kibbutzniks maintained that those afternoon hours from four to seven and all of Shabbat, the day of rest reserved solely for families, enabled fathers to spend more time with their children than most fathers in the city and suburbs.

In general, though, the kibbutz system was designed to maximize productivity in its working adults during the day and give parents plenty of time off from child-rearing in the evenings when they gathered together, unencumbered.

Apart from the few hours a day we kids spent with our parents, we were in the Children's House in sleeping rooms with children our age. We shared clothing, naptimes, and toys, and we traveled as a group, like a litter of pups. Kibbutz women assigned to the Children's House, not our moms and dads, took care of us. Parents even ate their meals separate from their children, which frustrated my father who wanted to see me more during the day. On one occasion he braved angry looks in the dining room when he brought me to sit with him at dinner. It baffles me that he was the only one to challenge this rule.

I can understand how being with your child for just a few concentrated hours a day could be appealing. Parenting within a short window of time has to be less frustrating than navigating a kids' needs and moods and desires, minute after minute, day after day. In a way it protected us. With so many people to support you and activities around as distractions, you might not ever have to know how you felt about your marriage, the fact that you were a parent, or even yourself.

Though I saw my mom and dad less than my Children's House group, the kibbutz was a comforting and easy place to grow up. I knew practically everyone and they knew me. My parents were where I expected to find them, and I knew I belonged. I always had kids my age to play with and plenty of people around who could take care of me, and I grew confident.

More than any other place I lived as a child the kibbutz felt like my home. I know this not only because I was happy there but because I felt so comfortable and safe; I never questioned it could change. And that is not something I've been able to do anywhere I've lived since. Maybe being able to take your family and home for granted is the surest sign you're winning in the childhood department.

My parents tell me when I was three, I'd often stop at neighbors' houses along the way home from the Children's House to ask for a treat or something to drink, or simply to say hello. On an afternoon when I was late, my mother asked each of the neighbors about me. One woman reported I had come by for a piece of chocolate. Another woman had given me a cookie. Yet another, a glass of water. This was only a two-block walk, so I know I couldn't have been actually hungry or thirsty, but I was food-motivated and probably a little pushy.

When we'd talk about the kibbutz my mother was always sure to tell me that I was the largest and tallest of the kids in my age group, and a bit of a character. She loved to describe how at mealtimes when one serving of chicken and couscous was enough for the other children, I needed a second. When those other kids were content with a single glass of fresh tomato juice, I easily knocked back two and probably could have handled a third.

According to my mother's memories of this time I asked for what I wanted, told people what I thought, and I always made it my business to inspect their homes. When we visited a friend of hers in Jerusalem one day, I took myself on a tour of her apartment, and when I wandered back into the living room, I said loudly in Hebrew, in front of the woman, "Mommy, her bathroom is *so* dirty!" My mother says her friend was embarrassed but that I was right, the apartment was a mess. She laughs when she tells these stories and seems a little bewildered by my forthrightness, probably partly because she couldn't have imagined having had this kind of confidence herself at such a young age.

My father used to tell me that when I walked into the room on the kibbutz the whole place lit up for him because, as he tells it, he was crazy about me. He seemed to be made for fatherhood, and he was; a natural teacher, explaining how things worked and answering my questions in as much detail as I wanted.

When he finished work for the day, he took me swimming at the kibbutz pool whenever he was able. In my grey-polka dotted bathing suit with a ruffle around the waist, I would jump into his arms and he would catch me, guiding me through the liquid world. Sunlight would flicker into the pool and shimmer against our skin, lighting up our bodies in segments, transforming regular life with its glimmer. In my father's arms I felt boundless. I could lose myself but still feel safe.

I liked when he was right next to me and he liked having me close to him. Together, we were a team. He let me watch him shave, and then I lathered up my own face with his shaving cream, the bristles of his brush prickling my face in the slippery foam. After he popped the razor blade out, I stroked the razor across my cheek as he did, happy to see the line the razor cut through the foam, the clean streak of skin underneath.

Though my father hadn't been able to serve in the U.S. military because of his poor eyesight, he got an assignment in the Israeli Army Reserves. Once when he was back for a few days from reserve duty he served every summer because he was a teacher, he showed me how to field strip an Uzi. There is a photo of me at three sitting in his lap helping him hold his Uzi, and another one on our front lawn, standing in my underwear in my father's boots. My curly, honey-colored hair blows across my forehead, and I look straight at the camera, assuming a powerful stance.

My father has always loved to remind me I'm a sabra, the Hebrew word for people born in Israel, named for the prickly pear that grows there and—as he liked to tell me when I was growing up—"tough on the outside, soft and sweet on the inside." Being tough was the part that appealed to me. I didn't see how being soft on the inside could help me, and when he'd say that part I squirmed. Toughness was what I prized.

There was only one time I can remember wanting to be small and depend on others to take care of me rather than taking care of myself. Just before my sister Nava was born when we celebrated Purim, I told my very-pregnant mother I wanted to be a baby. Purim is a Jewish holiday where people wear costumes and tell the story of Queen Esther who saved the Jewish people from the evil Haman. I was nearly three and very tall, but I sensed my time as the little one was nearly up and all that day I resisted speaking in full sentences. I wore a large cloth pinned around me like a diaper, a too-small bonnet-like hat jammed on my head, and insisted on drinking from a baby bottle. In photos I spill off my mother's lap, limbs overgrown and sprawling like the giant I was. It embarrasses me even now that I was unaware of how ridiculous I was, how obvious my need to be small and coddled was. To this day when I see kids pretend to be younger to get attention from their parents, I'm mortified.

But looking back, I'm also impressed. I knew what I wanted from my mother and I insisted she give it to me. It was one of the last times I'd ask this forcefully for her to take care of me.

~

On Lahav my father worked with the beef cattle and, for the first year, rode a tractor over the fields as he had envisioned; it was the adventure he had craved since his trainhopping and hitchhiking days. Every morning he jumped onto a kibbutz truck with some of the other guys and they dropped him off near the field he would plant, plow, or help harvest. He brought along a bag of oranges fresh from the kibbutz's orange grove, his pack of cigarettes, some jugs of water, and our dog, Auggie.

Alone in the fields under the sun, my father would ride his tractor scanning the horizon and the waving shafts of wheat. Auggie would follow the tractor row after row until he got tired or too hot, and then he'd find a spot of shade under a giant irrigation pipe and rest until the truck came to pick my father up for lunch. My father liked being alone like this. He had the land to think about and ideas for short stories he was beginning to work on and the adventure and thrill of knowing his life was unlike that of anyone he'd grown up with.

When his back started to suffer from the jostling of the tractor, kibbutz management moved him to livestock. He fed and took care of turkeys, whom he discovered act like, well turkeys. "Miserable creatures," he says to this day. Our kibbutz also had—and still has—the dubious distinction of being one of two kibbutzes that raised pigs—an animal deemed by Jewish law as completely unkosher. Because pig skin is so similar to human skin a researcher stationed at Lahav used pigs to test a salve for burns for soldiers, especially those in tanks whose combat wounds tended to be severe. The pigs would eventually become pork. To my chagrin, even now if I mention to an Israeli that I once lived on Kibbutz Lahav they get a funny look in their eye and, without missing a beat, blurt out, Kibbutz Chazer, the Piggy Kibbutz, and I nod quietly.

While my father enjoyed living in Israel, speaking Hebrew, and working with crops and animals, he disliked being told what to do and when to do it. He wasn't very social, unlike my mother who got together with friends on the kibbutz most nights. My father read novels and worked on the stories that were soon published in Jewish magazines in the US and in Israel.

My mother's reputation as a great cook followed her from their first kibbutz Gal-On to Lahav and she soon became head cook. She woke at 5:00 in the morning and headed to the kitchen to get the coffee started for all the kibbutzniks that were headed out to the fields and animal pens. Then she prepared giant vats of soups and filled industrial sinks with vegetables for that day's lunch and dinner. I can imagine her on mornings, groggy but dedicated, pulling on worn, comfortable clothes and shuffling across the narrow cement paths to the dining house to start her day, slowly becoming chattier as the sky lightened and more and more men and women arrived for their breakfast. I can see her greeting her co-workers, her movements becoming faster, more efficient as she hit her stride, calling out orders to the women working with her and getting food to the dining room on time.

My mother loved communal living. She longed for a sense of family and usefulness and the kibbutz suited her. At night she went to the social hall to meet friends, dance, play games, and perform skits with the drama group. She was totally supported by her community in a way she had never been when she was growing up. Connected to a network of industrious, like-minded women she could rely on to whom she felt closer in many ways than to my father, who could be possessive and headstrong much of the time. He was also jealous of the attention she got from men.

My father preferred the quiet of working at the kibbutz library; he was more interested in reading and writing than going to social events with her. My father also had a reputation among the women on the kibbutz as a pretty forward flirt. When my mother was pregnant with me, one of these women's husbands warned her about him. She didn't take his advice to heart.

One afternoon when she was in her third trimester with me she couldn't find my father anywhere on the kibbutz. She searched in the library, the dining room, and asked around but no one had seen him. Volunteers from other countries often stayed on the kibbutz for brief periods of time before they traveled on and that year, several young women had come from Holland. As my mother walked by their bungalows, she saw our dog Auggie, who followed my father everywhere, sitting on one of the young women's porches. She froze. Her heart began to race. She'd heard rumors of sleeping around over the years and most recently that a man from the kibbutz was having an affair with a Dutch woman.

She stood facing the bungalow, Auggie watching her and wagging his tail. She was light-headed. She backed away from the porch and went home.

Later that evening when she was washing up the dishes, she asked my father if he knew who was sleeping with the volunteer. He said he did.

"Who is it?" she asked, looking at him from where she scrubbed at the sink.

He shook his head. "I can't tell you," he said.

"Why?"

"Because. I can't tell you until we leave the kibbutz. I promise I'll tell you then."

I don't know why my mother didn't push my father more. Maybe she was afraid; maybe she wanted to believe him. She was pregnant with her first child, she had no resources of her own, and she was half a world away from Brooklyn and the friends who knew her best. I think she saw no choice but to trust him.

~

My parents say the entire eight years they lived on the kibbutz were peppered with discussions of going back to the States. When my sister was one and I was almost four, my parents made the decision to leave Israel for good. My father had been accepted at graduate schools in Connecticut, Indiana, Washington, and the University of Texas at Austin with generous scholarships. My mother didn't feel the need to be near her family and she had never been to the West Coast. When a friend recommended Seattle for its beauty and low cost of living, my parents chose the University of Washington. They reached out to Temple Beth Am in Seattle and when Ann, the temple president, got their letter she and her husband David agreed to host us while we got on our feet. My father would fly out to New York with my mother, Nava, and me first to settle us with my grandmother in Sheepshead Bay, Brooklyn for the summer while he got started in Seattle.

On the plane, my mother asked my father which man had been having the affair with the Dutch woman. While they soared west over the Atlantic my father said, "It was me."

I can imagine my mother buckled in her seat, baby Nava on her lap, her husband on one side, her four-year-old on the other, her body frozen as she tried to comprehend. He'd deceived her, then revealed the truth on his terms. Why hadn't she heeded the warnings? What do you do when the person you love, the father of your children, the one you're moving across the world with, admits he has betrayed you? How do you leave with a child on your lap and another right beside you?

First One to Leave

I moved to Washington State with my husband when my daughter was five months old. I had grown up mostly in New York City but had spent high school summers with my mother in Seattle. Those visits were a respite from my city life, from cockroaches and garbage piled up on street corners, from my life with my father and from the many months she and I had been separated. It was a promised land.

But years before that, Seattle was the first place my parents lived together in the US after leaving Israel. Moving there as an adult, with my fledgling family in tow, was more complicated than I had imagined it would be. I didn't realize how many memories would come rushing back from those early years of my childhood when I first understood my parents weren't happy.

Our first temporary home in Seattle was in Capitol Hill with the Temple Beth Am family willing to host us while we got on our feet. That is Ann and David, the parents, were willing to host us. Their two teenage sons and one teenage daughter seemed less than thrilled with the arrival of our disheveled family of four, crying toddler included, into their sprawling Tudor home. And I'm pretty certain they wanted nothing to do with me.

Neither did the fair, blonde girl who lived next door. Cynthia was like nothing I'd ever seen before. A white vision in a pink dress, she looked like a doll, with her platinum hair neatly combed and parted exactly in the middle of her scalp, held back from her creamy face with matching pastel-pink hairclips. She was six, a full two years older than me, but she was soft-spoken and petite, and her movements were graceful. She was like an alien species, or I was.

When I saw her, I immediately understood what I was not. I wasn't dainty, I wasn't delicate, and I wasn't quiet. Compared to her I was big and unkempt; uncouth. I talked with a thick Israeli accent and a pronounced lisp. And to top it off, when we'd stopped off in Brooklyn for the summer, I'd fallen off my Grandma Lina's bed and almost knocked my two bottom front teeth out. A dentist there fitted me with two silver caps that gleamed darkly in my mouth.

I knew whatever Cynthia had going on was out of my reach but that didn't stop me from pursuing her. I sought her out any time she was on her porch, but she didn't seem eager to talk to me. When I did get her to stop what she was doing and look at me she answered my questions with hesitation and never asked me to play with her or offered her toys. I couldn't seem to win her over, or her parents. They barely responded when I spoke, as if I were a strong gust of wind messing with their hair, whipping at their coats, and, if they just waited long enough, I would pass and they could get off their porch and go back inside to safety.

They were the only neighbors I met while we stayed at Ann and David's. Most of the time my mother, Nava, and I were on our own while my father was at school. Capitol Hill was a highly walkable neighborhood and close to Volunteer Park, which smelled of the cedar wood chips that covered the playground at the park, and the green, sappy scent of the ferns and rhododendrons that lined the play area. That August my mother took Nava and me to the wading pool to play in the sprinklers. I loved the smell of water and sun hitting the pavement, the sound of kids shrieking, and the warmth of the ground under my feet.

I felt more comfortable at the park exploring the dirt and flowers than I did at Ann or David's house, or trying to talk to Cynthia. But I still had a sense of myself being larger and sturdier than most kids. I knew I wasn't as cute and I certainly wasn't as affectionate as Nava. She cuddled you into submission even if you were busy doing something else. My parents called her "Monkey," and she was. She twisted and climbed and wound herself around my mother's legs and arms and wouldn't let go. Even if my mother started to get annoyed, Nava could melt her.

One summer afternoon about three weeks after we'd arrived, my family walked home from Volunteer Park together. "Up you go, Monkey," my father said, and scooped her into his arms for the rest of the way. It was one of those not too hot Seattle days when the sky is brilliant blue and the dogwood and elm trees vivid green.

Skipping alongside my parents, with the confidence of the eldest child, certain that my nickname would be even better, I said, "If Nava's Monkey, what am I?"

Silence.

My face was upturned, waiting for my animal.

My mother didn't exactly giggle; it was more of a smothered, muffled sound. Then she answered, "You're Donkey."

I stared up at her in silence. Donkey. Big-eared, big-mouthed, loud. Not a horse but the horse's squat, plodding, less graceful cousin. That's what I was? There was absolutely nothing cute about a donkey.

I had been the biggest baby on the kibbutz and I was still tall for my age and, as always, a hearty eater. My mother got a kick out of my appetite and told people when it came to food and me, she had to keep it coming. I listened closely, assessing what these stories meant and what my parents felt about me. When I was younger, I took these anecdotes as compliments. But as I grew up and my belly didn't fit neatly into the waistbands of my skirts and pants, when I had to safety pin instead of button the two sides together to get them to meet, I decided I was too big and too much as a person, unable to shrink even when I wanted to.

On the kibbutz, life had been casual; lots of kids were scrappy and sunbaked and free. But in Seattle, I felt I stood out. Seattle people were subdued. They didn't emote or express; they conserved their energy—for what I don't know—but I splattered over my edges. Here I was, this four-year-old with strange looking teeth and a double chin, an Israeli accent and Israeli demeanor: a certainty that the way I did things was right. On the kibbutz I had navigated, without a hitch, a world dictated by adults. Wherever I went people had seemed happy to see me, or at least amused. Maybe I was like the wacky sitcom neighbor who drops by unannounced but makes the scene more interesting. If I didn't like something, I spoke up. If I needed anything, I asked for it. A community had cradled me. I understood I was protected and looked out for, if not exactly by my parents, at least by their proximity and by the many adults minding the perimeter. It wasn't that I was personally cared for at all times, but at all times taken care of en masse. A kind of safety in numbers.

In Seattle, though the place was bigger and I was around new people all the time—at the grocery store, the park, the dentist, the ice cream shop—I really only knew my parents, so my mother and father counted that much more. I needed them all the time.

Back in Israel they didn't have to take care of Nava and me but for a few hours every afternoon. They had never been through the day-to-day challenges of raising kids on their own. Now they had to make meals and feed us, figure out what to do with us all day, put my sister back to bed when she woke through the night with no support whatsoever. They had left a village for a city and were now caught in a maelstrom of tasks and demands they had swapped our old life for, far from everyone and everything they had known. Without friends or family nearby to lean on, their day-to-day lives must have begun to feel bleak.

~

What I remember most about the first—and as it turned out the last—house my parents rented together in Seattle was how dimly lit it was, and how I could never get warm. I was born in Be'er Sheva, on the northern edge of the Negev desert where the several inches of rain that fell were mostly in January, and the temperature was in the seventies and eighties most months; the winter only about twenty degrees cooler.

It was autumn in Seattle, when the misty rain began to fall and continued most days. The sky was gray, the house was a wan yellow, and even the greens of the conifers looked washed out and faded. The streets were constantly attempting to dry out, the grass perpetually chilly and wet. When I walked through the yard, the toe box of my brown shoes darkened. While my room in the bright Children's House had felt welcoming with its sun-bleached walls and smooth yellow-tile, our Seattle house, its creaking wood floors and drafty windows in splintery panes, felt old and decaying, all harsh angles and shivers and bones. Our rental house was a sad house, in need of paint, in need of light, and too cold. It was here that what was wrong between my mother and father began to creep around the corners and fill the silences.

The first place the four of us lived on our own in America could have been where my mother and father embraced being parents and began building our family's life. Instead it was where the pain between them took root and spread, breaking their marriage, and ultimately our family, apart.

My father was gone more, teaching and studying, and conversations between my mother and him only concerned the daily schedule along with their exchange of goodbyes. The tension between them made him less playful but even so, my memory is that he still tried with me and Nava, reached out with his warmth, perhaps part of him understanding how little it would take from him to make things feel better for us.

On the mornings he left for the university I'd follow him into the kitchen where he would pause at the counter to take a last sip of coffee from his chipped beige mug. He ruffled my hair and I leaned into the warmth of him, my body perhaps understanding before I did that I didn't want to be in the house without him.

He'd pick up his leather briefcase, head for the door, and my face-watching vigil began: my eyes trained on my mother who stood apart from him as he said goodbye to her, my focus shifting to him to see if he was going to try to hug her, back to her to see if she was angry with him. I would turn away from her and run after him so I could have a kiss goodbye before he shut the door.

The house was quiet.

From our living room window, I could see older kids playing in the schoolyard across the street and that's where I wanted to be. I was still too young for school myself but I missed being with kids my age. The neighbor boy Jason who lived next to me played with me sometimes, but we didn't get along because he, unlike my friends on the kibbutz, wouldn't do exactly what I told him to do.

I was stranded in a chilly, wet city trying to learn how to live an American life and my mother, once a beaming, exuberant, and playful woman in charge of feeding hundreds of people was stranded in a house alone with two little kids, errands to run, and bills to pay. She and my father had decided she would stay home with Nava and me to ease our transition to our new life. But when I spoke with him years later, he told me he realized that my mother would have been much better off with a babysitter to watch us and a job to go to, so she could be out in the world.

My mother had moved away from the best home she had known to start again in Seattle, to support a man who had betrayed her, but who had offered her a kind of map to her future. A future that *looked* like something she could be satisfied with. But what she wanted was not there. Not in herself, not in her life. Perhaps she was wondering what, at twenty-eight years of age, she had made of herself, whether she could be a regular mother, a regular wife. She was considering whether she should leave.

I remember finding my mother and father on the sofa one evening after I was supposed to be asleep. I knew I shouldn't be out of bed, but I couldn't settle down and when I left my room I saw them sitting next to each other through the panes of the French doors in the living room. I watched them for a moment, sitting two feet apart, my father angled toward my mother, my mother looking ahead, both speaking in low voices. I was excited to see them talking. I had found evidence that they still liked each other. Proof that four-year-old me had been wrong about the uncomfortable feeling I lately had been getting whenever I was around them. They weren't in the same place often and I was so happy to see them there, side by side.

I opened one of the doors and stuck my head into the room, the wood floor creaking beneath my steps. As if I was expected, welcome even, I asked in the most sing-songy voice I had, like the comic relief making my entrance, "What are *you* two doing up so late?"

My mother didn't react, and my father just gave me a small smile. I wasn't sure they had really heard me.

I put my hand on my hip and leaned further in and asked, even louder this time, "I said, what are you doing up so late?"

It was only after I felt my words hang in the silent room that I saw how weary they looked. Nothing had changed in their expressions; they weren't glad to see me. My father, who was usually a fan of most anything I did, barely looked at me. His body still facing my mother, he glanced over only to say, in the most subdued tone I'd ever heard him use, "Go to bed, kid."

I backed out of the doorway, feeling foolish for not noticing the heaviness in the room—a feeling that was by now another member of our family.

~

I've spoken to my parents separately about this chapter of our lives and from what I can glean, my father wanted to prove that he could take care of Nava and me, so when my mother said she needed space he was the one who stayed on in the yellow house with us. He wanted us to live with him because he loved us. Also, perhaps he wanted to show my mother that if she was going to pull the plug on this life they had created together, he could not only land on his feet, he could be the better parent. My mother moved into her own apartment nearby in the same neighborhood and got a job in social service, working at Metrocenter YMCA. For the first time in my life I saw her only on the weekends.

I can't remember the moment she moved out and I don't know why, maybe it was too upsetting for me to hold on to, maybe because as with many aspects of my childhood, in our family we didn't discuss our feelings about big transitions much. In part that was the norm for the era in which I grew up—so different from largely accepted modes of communicating with children today, in which adults check in with kids and share their own emotions with them. The way my family coped was how I too learned to cope: we pushed through.

Between school and teaching, my father soon realized he was having a hard time caring for us full-time. He found an apartment and we began seeing *him* only on weekends, and my mother got to move back into the yellow house. She kept her YMCA job, Nava attended preschool, and I went to kindergarten and after school daycare until she picked me up. She cooked us homemade dinners every night, mostly healthy things like tofu and stir-fry vegetables, and she tried to teach us to eat with chopsticks. She served us plain yogurt with a dollop of raw honey for a treat and tried to buy everything fresh. To save money she shopped for bulk foods from the nearby co-op, with its drably clothed customers and bright piles of vegetables, and aromas of cumin and dried figs. To my child's eye the bins of beans and grains in all sizes and shapes resembled piles of different kinds of dust with scoops, but anything she made was delicious.

I was five years old, my parents newly separated, when my father took me out on weekends for one-on-one time that he called, "dates". He brought me to my first movie—*Star Wars,* when it was released, and he took me canoeing on Lake Washington. He told me I was the captain and let me decide which direction to go; every time I chose, and we cut a trail across the smooth steely water, he made a big deal about what a good job I had done navigating. Even though the lake was vast and I was small, I felt safe and brave because I was with him. My father moored me.

At least once a week he took Nava and me to Round Table Pizza for dinner. Outside the restaurant it was often drizzling and dark, the reflection of streetlights shimmering back from the wet asphalt of the parking lot, but inside the restaurant was filled with cushioned vinyl booths and polished wood and warm yellow lamps suspended over the tables. My father, calling on his Bronx upbringing, encouraged us to fold our slices of pizza down the middle and eat them with our hands. "Real New Yorkers eat it like this," he demonstrated. "It's a crime to eat pizza with a fork and a knife," he proclaimed, shaking his head at the Seattleites dining around us.

I knew I was part of the New York club and I was thrilled that we were special in this way. He continued to explain the intricacies of pizza to us while the servers with their homogeneously good Scandinavian looks smiled and brought around pans of different kinds of pies for us to try. I loved sitting back with my father on one side of me, Nava on the other, and picking out a slice of ham and pineapple, or black olives, mushrooms and green peppers, whatever was offered—having however much I wanted at least in this place, to feel satisfied.

The food and the noise of other people made dinnertime festive those nights, different from the dim and quiet rooms at home. I didn't want to ever leave. Inside I could forget about the drizzling night, the chill I'd feel as soon as I stepped outside. My father was animated, and the servers came to check back all through dinner. They fed us and took care of us, and I could forget my mother was missing from the table.

Maybe my father grew impatient or wanted to punish her, or maybe he couldn't live with the uncertainty of not knowing whether she'd ever decide to come back, but he soon took her by surprise and served her with divorce papers. When the lease on our first house expired, my mother found us another rental and she, Nava, and I moved into a pretty sky-blue house with yellow trim.

The summer before I turned six, soon after my parents' divorce became final, my father came to the door of the blue house holding his TV. He said he couldn't bring it with him when he moved to New Jersey, and he wanted us to have it. His flight was in the next few days so he had also come to say goodbye.

In the foyer, I saw him and my mother, speaking again in the low voices I'd come to fear. They didn't sound angry, but something wasn't right. I wanted to watch but was afraid to. I hadn't seen my parents talk together this way in a long time. From the living room, I peeked around the corner where the hallway began, my fingers holding onto the edge where the two walls met.

They were subdued, almost as if an invisible balloon between them was filling and filling as they talked, growing tauter after the end of each sentence. But there was also something gentle between them, and I didn't want to look away. I kept watching them where they stood, high up and away from me. I wondered if they loved each other again. If they would get back together.

Then whatever had been building up broke over them. I heard a low cry from my father, a sound like a wounded animal. His chest shook. His eyes behind his thick glasses were red and he was crying. He held onto my mother as if she alone could stop him from shaking. I watched my mother put her arms around him and she began to cry, too.

I went to where they stood, my father leaning on my mother, her arms bracing him, her body still but for the way his body wracked hers.

"What's wrong?" I asked, leaning into their legs.

"Daddy's going away," my mother answered.

"Where?"

"I'm moving to New Jersey," he said. His voice wasn't his voice; it was a smothered, choking sound.

I couldn't catch my breath. I held onto them, but they weren't making it better. They were letting pain spill over our lives again. I didn't know how to protect myself. They were all I needed but also what I had to escape.

I ran up the stairs to my room, as fast as I could, hoping I could outrun the sadness. I wouldn't see my father again for a year.

Newly Divorced Women

After my father left, my mother, Nava, and I went on living in the blue house and I started first grade. I still had silver caps on my bottom front teeth, I was loud, opinionated, and I had yet to lose my Israeli accent or lisp. I was the kind of kid that would drive *me* crazy. I'd met some of the kids in the neighborhood and I was hoping to be their friend, but they didn't seem to know what to make of me. Our conversations didn't go far and when I could get them to acknowledge me, I felt their hesitation when we talked. But, the more someone seemed uninterested in me, the harder I tried to draw them in.

I staged a bit of a coup one day after school that fall, and finally got the others to listen to me. I gathered my tentative pals around: a cute, tall, blond white boy two years older named Eric; a thin, Black girl with long, braided hair and buck teeth named Monique, also older; and a petite, long-haired, white girl with bangs, whose name escapes me but was most likely Heather. I had an idea to make money and I knew this was my way in. "We should start a business," I announced. What this neighborhood needed, I explained, was a design crew to help with all the thick ivy that clung to the houses.

"What we need to do," I said, "is take ivy from houses that have too much and use it to decorate houses that don't have enough!"

There was no response from my small group. They didn't look convinced. But they didn't say no, so I got Monique to get her parents' wheelbarrow from her garage. The kids then watched as I went to work on the first house, without consulting the owner, ripping out an armful of ivy amongst the ropes that had run up one side of the exterior. The other kids finally joined me, halfheartedly pulling out a couple of the vines and dropped them onto my pile in the wheelbarrow.

"Okay, it's time," I said, wiping my now-tender hands on my pants. "Who wants to ask that house?" I pointed to the Craftsman next door. They glanced back and forth at one another but didn't move. None of them wanted the job. "Don't be scared," I told them. "Look, I'll show you how."

The thin woman with mousy brown hair who answered the door looked confused by my offer so I explained it again.

"What we're doing is putting ivy wherever you want it. We can decorate your porch railing, your gate, we can put it anywhere!"

"What did you say?" she asked, squinting her eyes at me.

I repeated my vision for her home, this time emphasizing the twirls we could make around her banister but I could see I was losing her; animation left her features. Quickly, trying to ignore the shaky feeling that maybe I had made a mistake and was about to get in trouble, I put our landscape decorating on special; I *had* to get this woman to say yes so the kids could see my idea was a good one. For today only, I announced, I could give it to her for free. But it was too late; her face had already gone tight.

My group of decorators and I approached several more houses, but no one wanted us on their property and the kids lagged farther behind me. My brief glint of influence, my chance at leading like I had on the kibbutz, flickered out. Without talking about it, the neighborhood kids and I went our separate ways. I walked back to my house alone, the green smell of fresh-cut plants coating my hands, my stinging fingers chapped and sore from pulling tough tendrils out of stone.

~

33

On Saturday mornings I woke up early and settled in on our green secondhand loveseat to watch TV. I watched all the cartoons until they were over for the morning; shows like "The World's Greatest Super Friends", "Bugs Bunny", and "Challenge of the Super Friends." I didn't know what my mother was doing—sleeping or reading in her room—but she allowed me to watch for hours at a time. I was getting a crash course in what being American meant and most importantly, learning what kind of woman I wanted to be. I really liked a live action show called, "The Secrets of Isis" where the beautiful Isis with her long flowing brown hair summoned the winds with her goddess powers and rescued foolish high school students from an angry bear or a ring of car thieves. Like so many kids my age I was mesmerized by Wonder Woman, and the Lynda Carter live action show was my favorite. Nothing seemed better than being a powerful and beautiful superhero like her.

Except maybe working as a cocktail waitress. That was what I'd tell people when they asked what I wanted to be when I grew up. I had seen women serving drinks and food through the windows of the bars and restaurants we walked by on Capitol Hill, and I liked their shiny hair, glossy lips, and cute uniforms. I wanted to be made-up and glamorous like them and I had decided I would change my name to Cindy or Wendy or Tina as soon as I could. My own name caused trouble. People didn't know how to pronounce Ronit; often it didn't sound right in their mouths—they'd say Rah-nit, Rah-neet, or they'd mishear and call me Monique or Bernice—and I was beginning to dislike the way it drew attention to how different I was from other kids in Seattle. I wanted to know I'd grow up to fit in. That my lisp and my accent would be gone, that my potbelly and giant cheeks would shrink, that soon I'd have lots of friends. I wanted to know that despite how clunky I felt so much of the time, one day soon I'd be lovely.

If we went to a toy store I would head for the dress-up section right away. With a desire as strong as thirst, I'd paw through the pink purses and hard plastic high-heeled shoes with translucent toe straps, decorated in rhinestones or wispy pale pink feathers, hoping to find a pair that fit to complete my transformation into the most beautiful girl the world had ever seen. But when I tried them on, my feet were already too big for the kid sizes; my heels jutted inches past the end of the shoes. How had I missed the stage when I could have worn them? I must have skipped over being little.

I wanted to be a dancer or performer of some kind; someone who was the center of attention, so I practiced, relentlessly. My mother had turned the house's sunroom, its many windows facing the backyard, into a playroom for my sister and me. I would listen to and sing along with my record *Tina the Ballerina* about two hundred times a day, and I knew every word. I pirouetted around the small room in my nightgown, lose my balance, bump into the shelves where we stacked our toys and games, right myself, and start spinning all over again.

My mother also had music playing in the house most of the time. She'd blast Carly Simon's *Hotcakes* and *Anticipation* and Carole King's *Tapestry* through the speakers as if we were all newly divorced women, bathing our house in sound, as if we really were going to make it on our own. We didn't talk about my mother's single status but the lyrics seeped into me. I'd move through the rooms listening to these powerful, long-haired women singing to me, pore over their photographs on their album covers and try to decide who was the prettiest. I was yet to formally join the single woman sisterhood, but in time it was clear I'd be there. That was what happened to women, I believed; that's where you ended up if you were strong and you knew yourself. You went it alone, just like my mother was doing now that my father was gone. I didn't know then that this wasn't really who she was; that what she truly yearned for was freedom from the life she was now living. She didn't want to be on her own at all and she would soon find a community to enfold her so that she wouldn't have to be.

Enter Bhagwan

Though I almost never got sick, one morning during the winter of first grade I woke up with chills and a sore throat. My mother put her hand on my forehead and pursed her lips when she felt how hot I was. She told me she'd take the day off but first she would have to drop my sister off at preschool. I'd stay by myself, she said, until she returned in a little bit.

"Hop into my bed," she said and covered me with her blankets. She tucked them up to my chin and smoothed them out.

"Do you want some tea?"

"Okay," I nodded.

She ran her thumb across my temple and back again like I remembered her doing at times when we lived on the kibbutz. The lights were off and the room was grey-lit from the overcast day. I saw the leaves on the maple tree outside her window rustle in the wind and watched her face while she moved my hair away from my cheek. She didn't rush or hurry out; she didn't look frustrated. I settled deeper into the mattress while she talked to me in gentle tones, as if I needed special care. She put *Sesame Street* on the TV for me and left me in the house but I wasn't scared to be alone; I wasn't worried that she wouldn't come back. I felt cozy in her bed, certain that even though she had gone out, she had me in mind. It was the softest day.

But there were hard days too, days when I had trouble finding evidence that she wanted to mother me or even liked having me around. Late that fall, an invisible force furrowed her brow and stiffened her jaw; there was a noticeable shift in her appearance that made me nervous. I thought she looked mad, perhaps mad at me. Her eyes seemed to be focused on something I couldn't see. I don't know whether it simply didn't occur to her to mask what she was going through around me, or whether she had no idea how to do so. I don't think there was space left inside her to reach across and let me know I didn't have to worry, that we would be okay no matter what.

Her unhappiness began to simmer, her frustration threatening our life together. When I was an adult, she confirmed that having to care for me and my sister on her own after having had a kibbutz community to rely on for so many years made this one of the bleakest times in her life. She became afraid that she would physically hurt us the way her mother had hurt her.

When I was a new mother and home with my daughter those first few weeks after my husband had returned to work, I felt anxious, and at times as if I were alone at sea with my baby, with no one to rely on or even tell me what to do next. I imagine my mother's frustration and uncertainty in Seattle in the late 1970s were far worse than mine, and potent enough to trigger the long-dormant loneliness she hadn't experienced since childhood, when her mother ravaged her emotionally.

When my mother first moved to Seattle with my father, she didn't even know how to write a check. Now she was almost thirty and alone, working as much as she could at Metrocenter YMCA, and trying to take care of her daughters by herself with no relief but the child support payment my father kept up every month.

The more discontent she grew, the more time she spent listening to tapes by Bhagwan, the guru her new friend, Jim, had introduced her to. The more sannyasins she became friends with, the more India beckoned.

One afternoon that winter, the doorbell rang when I was alone downstairs. Nava was asleep and my mother was in her room again with the door closed, and I wasn't supposed to bother her. I didn't know who it could be because we rarely had visitors, but I hated when she was up in her room and the house was so quiet. I went to the front hall, unlatched the lock, and opened the door. A man with dirty blond hair I'd never seen before was standing in front of me.

"Is your mother home?" he asked, smiling at me in a kind but insistent way.

I stared back from the doorway, not sure how to answer. She had told me not to disturb her but now somebody else wanted her. Maybe *he* was allowed to bug her. I didn't know what to do but since I was having a hard time being on my own this was a perfect excuse to interrupt her, and I seized on it.

"I'll go get her!" I told the man and left him downstairs. I hurried up the staircase, worried she'd be angry, but thrilled at being able to get her out of her room. Anyway, I decided, if she were going to get mad it would be mostly at the stranger, not me.

As soon as I got to the top of the stairs, I heard the muffled sound of Bhagwan's recorded voice from behind the door. She had begun listening to the cassettes whenever she was in her room. To me it felt as much like an invasion as if an actual man was there with her, a stranger she'd invited into our home without introduction.

I stopped in front of her bedroom door and put my ear up to it to hear.

"I speak to seduce you into silence," he crooned. "I use words so that you can be persuaded towards the wordless existence…"

My body recoiled. I hated the way he lingered on the soft c in "existence," how slowly he talked. How could my mother listen to someone so boring?

I steeled myself and knocked on her door.

"Right now," the tape went on, "you cannot understand silence, you can only understand words. I will have to use words to give you the message of silence…"

She didn't answer. I knocked again.

"…And if I am to help you, I have to come close to you. Before you can come close to me, I will have to come close to you—that is the only way."

The tape stopped.

"I told you I was resting," she grumbled.

"But there's a man downstairs," I said and held my breath.

There was silence.

"I didn't know if it was important."

I stood in the dark hall, unsure what to do next. I chewed on the inside of my cheek and waited.

She opened the door.

"I didn't know what to do," I said trying to make eye contact with her but she looked away and brushed by me on her way down. I stole a glance at her candlelit room, the shades drawn, sandalwood incense burning, wondering what other mysteries it held. But she was already making her way down so I followed her as quickly as I could.

The man was only trying to sell her something, and she sent him away. She stayed downstairs after he left, which is exactly what I had wanted but not how I pictured it. She was distant, her mind somewhere else. I couldn't seem to engage her.

Her attention was focused on what Bhagwan was offering: connection and belonging to something radical, with a greater purpose than merely her family. Nava and I needed her more than we needed anyone, but she needed something else.

Maybe my mother thought she'd be better off single and free when she and my father separated, but I don't know that she was cut out for that. She had never been by herself. She went from her mother's house, to the farm in New Jersey, to Kibbutz Lahav.

The kibbutz, apparently, is where she wanted to return.

After my father moved to Newark my mother wrote to Lahav and asked if she could come back with Nava and me. On the kibbutz she'd once again have childcare, a school for her kids, a home, and a community to support her. She wanted the three of us to first visit Bhagwan's ashram in India and then settle in Israel. But the kibbutz declined. In their letter, they said the kibbutzniks had been split when they voted on the decision; that really there was no room on Lahav for my mother, a single woman with children. I wonder now if the other families were concerned about having an unattached lady in their midst, worried that she would be a threat or a burden.

How ironic: my father was the one who'd cheated while they lived there, yet my mother was the one who was not allowed to return. If the kibbutz had said yes, perhaps she wouldn't have found the promise of security and empowerment that Bhagwan offered so appealing. Perhaps I would have spent the rest of my childhood with her.

Plans for the Summer

My mother still planned to spend the summer at Bhagwan's ashram in Pune, India, and she was thinking of taking Nava and me with her. She didn't seem to realize that in Pune, Bhagwan encouraged sex as a means for sannyasins to discover their true spiritual nature—or that he saw children as a hindrance. I'm not sure how she missed that when she read his books and listened to his tapes. In the research I've done his stance is glaringly clear.

That spring my mother called my father with a request for him to take Nava and me for the summer. At the time he was living in Newark, New Jersey with his girlfriend Tracy, whom he'd met in Seattle, and her two teenage daughters in a small two-bedroom apartment in the Ivy Hill housing projects in Newark. He was doing public relations work for a Jewish nonprofit while trying to write, as he said only a little jokingly, "the great American novel."

Lucky for me and Nava my father absolutely did not want us going to India. Between potential diseases we had not encountered before and the unknowns of the ashram he thought it was a bad idea. My mother's new friends in Seattle cautioned her against bringing us, too, so she asked a mom friend of hers to take us for the summer. But after that friend changed her mind my mother called my father again.

This was after dinner and Nava was already asleep. I was at the kitchen table brushing my ballerina Barbie doll's ratty, tangled hair. She had been a fifth birthday present from Ann and David when we first lived with them in Seattle and I cherished her. I had named her Tiffany and she had a white tutu, plastic ballet shoes, and a tiara that shined in the light. She had long, smooth brown hair, the kind I wanted to have, but it was badly knotted now. I didn't understand how it had turned so dull and clumped. I worked through the knots with my hairbrush while my mother talked to my father on the phone.

"I can place the girls in foster care with Jewish Family Services while I'm gone," she said. She looked over at me while she listened to what my father was telling her. "I'm definitely going to go...No, *this* summer." She stood at the sink with the phone, facing me.

"What is it, Mom?" I asked.

She sighed and looked up at the ceiling. "Uh huh...well, if you can't take them...Hold on—" That's when my mother covered the yellow receiver and whispered to me, having prepped me for this beforehand. "Hang on, Ronit's here," she said and put me on the line with him.

"Hi Daddy," I said looking at my mother who held the phone to my ear. "Hi kid!"

My mother nodded for me to go on. "Mommy is going to India. Can we stay with you?"

My father let out a long sigh. "No, honey," he said. "I'm afraid there's no room here."

I turned to my mother. "He says there's no room."

"Ask him if Aunt Ellen can take you," she whispered.

"Can Aunt Ellen take us?" I repeated, his rejection of Nava and me competing with my sense of duty to my mother.

"I'm afraid not, honey."

I paused to listen to my mother's instructions. I held the phone in my left hand and twisted the coily phone cord around the fingers of my right hand. "How about Grandpa Sammy?" I only vaguely knew who these relatives I was asking to live with were, but I was nothing if not determined to help find a solution to my mother's problem.

"No, honey."

My mother whispered to me, and I repeated what she'd said. "Grandma Doris?"

"She's not well."

I held the phone to my ear and looked to my mother. My father was quiet on the other end, and my mother's brow was furrowed.

He said, "Put your mom on the phone, kid."

He told my mother that we could stay with him.

I was excited to go to the airport. Though I'd flown from Israel to New York and from New York to Seattle, I had no memory of being on an airplane. I liked the idea of my mother, Nava, and me taking a trip together, without her Bhagwan recordings to distract her, moving as a family through a large crowded place with so many other people on journeys. We had our bags and my mother had Nava, who carried her plastic doll, Naked Baby, by the hand—and we were going to visit my father. The closer we got to seeing him the more I felt the ache from his year-long absence.

When we stopped at the airport shop, my mother bought me a pack of Lifesavers for the flight. It was the first time I could remember her buying me artificial candy from a store like I'd seen other moms do for their kids. I stared at the bright colored stripes on the package as we walked to our gate. If I hadn't already been happy about air travel, this sealed it.

I didn't have much more than this on my mind as we flew east: being close to my mother and Nava for the whole flight, and the fact that I'd see my father when we landed. My chest fluttered thinking about it. Reuniting with him overshadowed the other part of the arrangement; the fact that my mother would be leaving us. What was on my mind was how I was going to make my Lifesavers last and whether my father would think I looked more grown up. Maybe it's lucky that a kid's brain can both compartmentalize like that and not fully comprehend some things. I didn't truly grasp this was goodbye.

The Prickly One

"Let's go Ronitchik," my father said, reaching his hand out for me. I hadn't heard this Yiddish pet name since the last time I'd seen him, the previous year. Taking his hand meant leaving Newark airport, which I wanted to do—everything about the place was jarring—the florescent lighting, the voices on the airport intercom, the reunions and separations happening all around us—but going with my father also meant leaving the place where I'd last seen my mother.

My mother, the person my life and heart revolved around, whom I'd calibrated myself to, even when I couldn't seem to reach her, had walked away the moment before. My father, whom I loved but only vaguely remembered, was holding my hand.

Sound had a muted but also echoey quality in the crowded terminal—voices speaking Hindi, Spanish, Korean, Japanese, and English swirled around me. I didn't want to go yet; I wanted my mother to turn around. I wanted to be there to wave goodbye again when she did so I could show her that I was still there. But I had lost her in the crowd.

My throat felt like it was closing.

My eyes stung.

I was so tired.

Carrying our small suitcases, my father weaved through the airport and guided Nava and me outside to find a taxi. I followed him as closely as I had followed my mother when we landed, keeping my eye on him but trying to take in everything else.

The smell of gas and cigarette smoke struck me as soon as we got to the street. Horns honked and taxi drivers shouted at each other; car doors slammed. Newark was much dirtier than Seattle—cigarette butts and wrappers flecked the oil-stained asphalt—and the air was hot and damp, like someone had wrapped me in a wet towel.

I stayed alert on the taxi ride to Ivy Hill, while my father chatted with the cab driver, watching lit-up rectangular building after lit-up rectangular building whip by. I'd never seen so many apartments or so much identical brick before.

Our taxi pulled up in front of a sprawling fourteen-story building set back from the sidewalk towering in the darkness, and the driver got our luggage out from the trunk.

Ivy Hill was not how I had pictured it. Ivy suggested green and residential, secluded and pretty, like in Seattle. But when we arrived that first night from the airport, the rows and rows of windows glowing yellow in the night were the only thing that gave an indication of warmth. I didn't think I was in danger, exactly, but I felt small. I wanted to huddle near someone, burrow into something. But I didn't move closer to my father; he wasn't who I wanted.

He hauled our suitcases up the walkway, and Nava stayed close to me as we stepped into the elevator; a metal box painted maroon that was quiet inside except for the noise of machine gears as we moved up. The quality of sound was dull and far away, as though someone had pressed their hands against my ears.

I suppose my father and his girlfriend Tracy chose Ivy Hill out of all the places they could have lived, because of its subsidized rents and its proximity to the city. It was cheap and he didn't have a lot of money. He worked for a Jewish nonprofit in the city that provided education and technical training to Jews around the world. Whenever he could, he focused on his novel and did freelance jobs in his spare time, working as a ghost writer for sex therapist and radio show host Dr.

Ruth Westheimer and other writers.

When Tracy and her two daughters—Sarah, sixteen and a high school sophomore, and Janine, thirteen and an eighth grader—greeted us at the door, Sarah smiled as if she'd been told to; Janine grudgingly said hello. Tracy welcomed us in but I wasn't too tired to miss the girls' lack of enthusiasm when Nava and I stepped inside.

My father had met Tracy in Seattle and followed her out to New Jersey. She was a small, subdued Japanese American lady who had been interned in a camp with her family just after the bombing of Pearl Harbor. She had grown up and married a Jewish man, converted to Judaism, and was now divorced. She chain-smoked like my father—Virginia Slims for her, Winstons for him, and cooked delicious meals. Just before Nava and I arrived, when she and my father had to acknowledge we were actually coming, she'd picked up a garage-sale dresser for us and placed it in the hallway outside the bedroom we would share with her daughters. And, she'd purchased two sets of bunk beds to replace Sarah and Janine's single beds so that Nava and I could sleep on the bottom, and the big girls could take the top bunks in the same narrow bedroom.

Though I was impressed with the freedom that seemed to come with their ages, I didn't like having two teenagers in charge of me. I was prickly from the beginning, making fun of Janine behind her back, sticking my tongue out at her when she left the room. I was too mature and composed to act like a younger kid, or even my age, but also not old enough to be considered or behave like anything but a little girl. Until then my role was "big sister," but now I was automatically "little sister," though I knew I could never be truly little—Nava was the certified baby of the family. The older girls told her what to do and she listened to them, while I became increasingly unhappy being the odd one out. I may not have loved spending that much time with Nava—she often annoyed me—but I certainly didn't want other people claiming her.

She was only four years old, game for anything and adorable, with round cheeks and big green eyes. She still sucked her thumb and played with stuffed animals and loved to cuddle. She was easy to read, easy to love. I didn't feel easy to love and as the weeks accumulated and my mother didn't call, I began to worry that I was easy to forget.

~

Nava and I had been in Ivy Hill for two weeks, and Tracy and I hadn't yet formed a connection. Part of me wanted this woman in my father's life to like me, but part of me was wary of her. One Saturday afternoon when Sarah and Janine were out with their father, Tracy announced that we were all going to take naps. I probably looked at her like she'd twisted her head all the way around. I was not a napper, and the idea of one was absurd to me. I didn't stop during the day, I went and went, my antennae fully extended collecting information and evaluating the people around me. To sleep and rest, to stop at all during waking hours was against nature as far as I was concerned. I could think of nothing worse than to lie in bed with the shades drawn, blocking out the daylight and the world outside, stuck only with my racing thoughts. Quiet time might mean feeling how I missed my mother and wondering whether she missed me.

I stared back at Tracy, my lips pressed together hard, my eyes steady. Tracy usually wore a thick mask of makeup: lots of foundation and powder, lipsticks in coral and pinks, and penciled-in eyebrows because her own were gone from decades of plucking. But today her face was bare. Without her makeup I could see her sunspots and age spots. Her face was imperfect and tired, not pretty. I didn't like how lifeless she looked, how unfinished; it agitated me.

I didn't know why my father wasn't part of this conversation. Had he heard about this plan? Where was he anyway? I knew he wouldn't make me nap if I didn't want to. I let my eyes slide past Tracy's head, through the slightly open bedroom door behind her, where I heard his typewriter. I wanted to call to him so he could come out and tell Tracy she was mistaken, and I could do whatever I felt like.

But I didn't call for my father. I took care of it myself. "I don't want to," I said. I had every reason to believe she would back down.

"That's what we're doing," she said.

47

I heard the tap, tap of his typewriter, the bell ring with the carriage return. He was obviously not getting involved.

"How long?" I asked, keeping my eyes steady on her.

"For a little while. Your sister is already in bed. You both need to rest."

I seized on "little." That was my way around it since little was subjective. I could handle a little. I shuffled into our bedroom, and Tracy closed her bedroom door. It was not quite dark enough to sleep, with the sun twinkling through slats of the venetian blinds and on the sides where they were not flush with the window. It was also too quiet.

"Nava," I said, rolling to face her. "Nava?"

"Yeah?" she said, looking up from cuddling Naked Baby.

"We can get up soon."

She smiled at me, staring back from where she lay.

I had no clock or watch in the bedroom with me. I had no idea what time it was or what time it had been when I first lay down. Nava could have used the nap; she probably would have fallen asleep within seconds if I had left her alone, but I didn't want to defy Tracy by myself. After what seemed like enough time, I said, "Let's go," and held out my hand for her. "We can't make noise. We don't want to wake them up."

Holding Naked Baby Nava followed, trying to tiptoe, her shoulders hunched up by her ears to make her body as small as she could.

We crept out of the room and down the hallway that led to the other side of the apartment. The ratty wood floor groaned beneath us. We took another step. We just had to get to the living room, and I could switch on the TV like I used to do in Seattle when my mother was in her room. I would keep the volume low.

Suddenly, Tracy opened her bedroom door. "Nap time is not over. Get back into the room."

"You said a little while. It's been a little while."

"It's only been a few minutes. That's not long enough."

I crossed my arms over my chest. "When's long enough?"

I didn't like adults who took breaks, who closed up for a few hours or shut off and were unavailable. And I didn't like quiet rooms. Staring at Tracy's worn out expressionless face, a part of me woke up and shifted inside. Besides Nava, my father was the only person in the apartment I was related to, and he wasn't helping me. I didn't know why he was letting Tracy tell me what to do.

Tracy got me to go back into my room that time, but afterwards I spoke with my father and I didn't have to nap again. His siding with me was a win but it looked like I would have to stay alert in my new living situation. It would be up to me to hack out a place for myself.

Every night when Janine crawled into her bed above mine, she switched on her little AM transistor radio, the sound at an almost indiscernible volume. On the rare nights I was still awake when she came in, I'd fall asleep straining to hear the song or trying to pick up the next note, a kind of meditation that lulled me. I would never have dreamed of touching the radio or asking her to turn it up; I knew I was a visitor in her world. It was grown-up to have your own radio that you could control and it underscored the difference in our ages even more. She had independence; I was a child stuck with the choices the adults around me made.

One day, about a month into our summer visit, I was in Tracy and my father's bedroom sitting at his desk and playing with his stapler. I was trying to see if it was possible to staple skin or if the stapler would only work on paper, and I got a staple partially lodged in my thumb. Not the smartest move on my part but I was surprised by how easy it was to hurt myself if I wanted to.

My father pulled the staple out of my thumb and washed it, talking to me about cleaning wounds as he did. This was the first time he'd taken care of me since he'd left the year before and he seemed calm and focused, totally competent. I watched him open up a Band-Aid and put it on my thumb without even a wrinkle in the bandage. It was comforting to watch him handle my injury with such confidence and I felt myself letting my guard down. After he'd applied the Band-Aid, I followed him to his bedroom and sat on a goldish-yellow, polyester bedspread and watched him pull on his socks. The apartment was quiet. I didn't know where anybody else was.

Over the last weeks, I'd felt myself growing a little more comfortable with this tall man with the long toes sitting next to me. I'd been close with him on the kibbutz, but when we moved to Seattle and my parents separated, we'd spent more time apart. Then he left for New Jersey. Did I really know him anymore? Hadn't he left Nava and me in Seattle?

My mother gave birth to me. I understood how I was part of her and people had said I looked like her. But this man could be any man. I didn't truly sense what we shared. How could I be certain I was connected to him? Because we were acting like it? Having been separated from him for nearly a year gave me some objective distance. In that moment sitting on his bed, I partially floated above myself to look down on the scene, and I felt how he was a stranger to me. How did I really know he was my father? How do you know you belong to someone? People make a bargain to take care of one another, but they can just as easily decide not to do so anymore. What if he'd said no, he wouldn't take us that summer? What if he decided he didn't want a relationship with us?

In fact, thinking about it now, had my mother not decided to take a trip of her own that summer to follow her guru, I can't say when we would have seen my father next.

The six of us were like a science experiment in that small apartment, especially the four of us kids stuck in that tiny room—like beached and wobbling jellyfish stranded on land, easy to prod, easy to disturb. At sixteen Sarah was thin, with smooth unblemished skin and shiny, straight long hair and wispy bangs. She moved in a measured way holding her back ramrod straight, as if her neck and torso had been fastened to a pole. The sleeves of the pastel blouses she wore were too short for her long arms, her slender wrists poking out of the cuffs. In keeping with her own growing commitment to Orthodox Judaism, she wore long skirts every day.

Mainly keeping to herself, Sarah smiled only occasionally, but I felt better when she did. She was the oldest teenager, my alpha whether she realized it or not, and I looked up to her. She was the one whose opinion I cared about. I listened to whatever she said, especially if it was directed to me. I also made sure to stay clear of her so as not to annoy her any more than my being there already did, hoping she might decide I was not too bad after all.

To Sarah I was probably like a wafting gnat, but to Janine I was more mosquito, a relentless invader. Janine was older than me but still young enough and insecure enough for me to sass and compete with. There was no way I was going to cede control to this depressed-looking and clearly awkward middle-schooler, so I gave her trouble.

"You use too much toothpaste," she told me when she passed the bathroom and I mouthed the words behind her back clowning for Nava. "We have to go," she called from the front door where she waited for me to put my cereal bowl in the sink, and I scrunched up my face and exaggerated her words in a whisper on my way out of the kitchen. Whenever she said anything that seemed to me like a directive, I mocked the way she talked. I didn't think for a minute that I had to listen to her or respect her; I had a mean streak and around Janine I let it out.

Whereas Sarah had delicate features and a quietness that approx.-imated grace, Janine appeared jagged and unsettled, as if she had been tossing in her bed all night, unable to rest. Janine had acne and frizzy hair that never shined. It was coarse and didn't style the way she wanted it to. No matter what she tried, it stuck out on the sides. I saw how she could maybe be pretty, but she cried a lot, and that made her skin blotchy, her eyes small and distant.

Sarah may not have been happy either but at least she kept her unhappiness to herself. Janine was so raw, so tender, it made me want to hurt her. She wore on the outside what I didn't want to admit I was feeling on the inside and it repelled me. In addition to that I had this idea I was leaving Ivy Hill and its cockroaches as soon as the summer was over. I was lucky because I had an escape plan; I could burn bridges because I didn't need these people. I had a mother I belonged to and a whole other life I was going to get back to in a few months. Tracy, Sarah, and Janine might be stuck in this apartment but I would get to leave. In many ways I was flipping them the bird from the moment I got there.

Still, despite my variously mixed feelings, I desperately wanted to imprint on a female figure and had no other choices but these women I now lived with. I wish we had gotten along better.

The months went by and I still could not figure Tracy out. Like her oldest daughter, Tracy smiled sometimes, but, unlike Sarah, whose eyes held no deep mystery, Tracy had a faraway look. I believed she either didn't like me at all or didn't know what to do with me, or both in different proportions at any given time. Maybe she was just busy with a demanding job in Manhattan, grocery lists to take care of, dishes to do, and worries I couldn't understand at the time.

Decades later when I was writing this book, I learned my father was still occasionally in touch with Tracy and that she lived in Seattle, same as me. I was surprised she never reached out or expressed interest in seeing me again. Even though I was grown with children of my own it still bothered me—hurt my feelings, really. Our relationship had been forced but I was sorry this woman who had played a maternal role in my life for several years wasn't interested enough to reach out, or even curious enough to ask after me. When I mentioned that to my father, he shrugged his shoulders; he didn't have an answer. At least not one he wanted to share.

The Shape of Family

One night that July, Tracy and my father told us to get our shoes on; we were going across the street to Ivy Hill Park. It was eight o'clock and not too hot now that the sun was down; just pleasantly warm. There was no chill in the air like there could be in Seattle on July nights. Here summer felt like a heated silk scarf swirling around my body, like I was drifting along on a current that buoyed me, that eased my shoulders away from my ears and slowed my gait.

Kids and young adults in the park were lounging on benches in the twilight, propped up against the wrought iron fence, balancing competing boom boxes on their shoulders that blared and thumped.

I stayed close to my father, the six of us streaming into the blurry maze of pathways and hard benches, headed toward the swings and a sandbox. It was an adventure to be out so late in the safe shape of a family.

Crickets began chirping after the sun went down and lightning bugs revealed themselves to me for the first time. They flickered on, flickered off; flickered on flickered off, like magic. The day was over, but the Mr. Softee ice cream truck came by, and my father and Tracy let each of us get a treat. I chose my favorite, soft-serve vanilla with chocolate sprinkles, and for the first time that summer—the first time in longer than I could recall—I had the feeling that this was where I was supposed to be, with all of us together.

My ice cream in hand, the five of us together in the sweet night, I let down my guard. Being part of a pack, out here in the world, gave me a sense of belonging. We stayed out until all of us were ready for home and nobody made me do anything I didn't want to; it was my night as much as it was anyone's. I was happy.

~

My mother was supposed to return to take us back to Seattle for the start of the school year. We had talked once since she'd gone to India, but she was at the ashram and communication was unreliable. Knowing I was going to see her in a handful of weeks and leave Ivy Hill behind fortified me.

But at the end of August, she let our father know she would not be returning, at least not anytime soon. I don't know how their conversation went; he shielded me from it. I can imagine his frustration, though. Maybe my mother's absence from our lives had been tolerable so far because he'd perceived it as finite. The idea that it would go on, the anger and helplessness of not being able to make her pick us up, must have sent him into a rage. He probably wanted to yell at her, to beg and threaten, but knew he had to be patient. You can't force someone to come back when they don't want to.

"You're going to stay here for second grade," he told me when he called Nava and me into the living room to talk. "Your mother is staying in India for a while." I knew even before he told us that something was wrong. I was beginning to develop a sixth sense for bad news; or had at least learned it was often around the corner when you least expected it. I wouldn't have wanted to be the one to say these words to me. To try to explain that my mother loved me but had decided to live in another country with her beloved guru instead of with her children. How could both be true?

So, it came to pass that right after Labor Day my father walked me the few blocks to Mount Vernon Elementary School on his way to work. I had on a backpack and was holding his hand. I don't know if he was able to see what was happening to me the closer we got to the school, how I felt like I was shrinking. I had been chatting with him when we first left the apartment, but now my voice felt stuck inside of me.

We walked past the school, its windows wrapped in navy blue security grates, and weaved around clusters of screeching children, who seemed much older than me. Girls with spiral braids, beaded cornrows, and fancy hairstyles I had never tried. My hair was down, as usual, with a headband which was the only way I knew how to wear it. We entered through the tall, metal doors and kids rushed by us into the building, their sneakers squeaking on linoleum.

Time slowed down as my father consulted the letter he was carrying to see which classroom I was in. I stood close to him, hoping he had made a mistake and that I wouldn't have to start today.

"Let's ask in here," he said, walking a few feet down a hall and toward an office that smelled like mimeograph ink and coffee. Before we could step inside, a woman with plum lipstick popped her head out and asked, "Can I help you?"

We followed her directions to my classroom around the corner and when we got there, children were already lined up. They started filing in and my heart jumped. I wasn't ready.

"Here you go, honey," my father said as he walked me over to my teacher, Mrs. Johnson.

I knew he had to go to work. I was supposed to say goodbye to him now; he was trying to say goodbye to me. But my chest hurt like it was being squeezed and I couldn't breathe properly. I began to cry.

"It's okay, honey, you're going to be okay," he said. He knelt down and I saw the kids still in the hallway watching me, but I didn't care. I was clutching onto my father, and sobbing, unable to speak. The months of trying to be okay without my mother poured out of me.

"Please don't leave," I begged him, "please don't go."

"It's going to be alright," he said, hugging me. He smoothed my hair down and wiped my cheek. In his eyes I saw his concern, his regret, and also his resignation. I knew that my crying was not going to change anything. This would end with him leaving for work and me staying here. And I could not tolerate it. My body shook; I hiccupped air. I kept trying to tell him to wait, but I couldn't get the words out. I was no longer in control of myself.

A year ago, I had said goodbye to my father when he moved to New Jersey. Two months ago, I had said goodbye to my mother when she left for India. What if he did what my mother had done and never came back?

Meanwhile, Back at the Ashram

When my daughter and son were ten and eight years old, respectively, my father brought me four books on Bhagwan. Each had a photo of Bhagwan's face on its cover, his long salt and pepper beard, his big glistening eyes draped with heavy lids.

"You can have these," he said.

"Not one, but four fun-filled volumes of guru mind-control and manipulation," I said flipping through the stack. "Thanks, Dad!"

"Aw, come on," he said, "I thought you might want them."

He was right; in a way I did. But, in a way I didn't.

He had bought the books decades ago at The Strand bookstore when he was trying to understand more about what had drawn my mother to the guru. At the time he thought he might write a book about Pune and Rancho Rajneesh. Now he was passing them on to me. I wonder if giving them to me was equal parts helping me do research and finally removing them from his life. I'm sure letting them go must have felt good.

The books included three volumes of the many talks Bhagwan had given, as well as *The Ultimate Game* by Kate Strelley. Touching them almost seemed risky. Welcoming them into my house felt in a way like inviting Bhagwan here, and I had sworn when I was a teenager not to ever utter his name. Looking at the covers felt kind of like discovering that a dream I had had was real, and that others had been there too.

I thanked my father for bringing them and, when he left, hid them behind other books on my bookshelf where I willed myself to temporarily forget about them. I knew I'd open them eventually.

I'm not sure what I thought would happen if I learned more about Bhagwan and his ashrams. My family had moved on as best we could since those days: Nava lived in Los Angeles with her family, I lived in Seattle with my husband and kids, my mother lived about five minutes away from me and my father split his time between New York and Seattle. After all of our relocating, we'd ended up in the very city where we'd last lived as a family.

What's more, when my father was in town, he and my mother and my husband and kids spent Shabbat dinner with each other Friday nights. My mother even cooked for us and my kids didn't give much thought to their grandparents being divorced. We carried on mostly without anyone questioning the peculiarity of the arrangement except for my father, who at almost every Shabbat dinner told us what an amazing cook my mother was and how she was known for her cooking on the kibbutz. And once a year, without fail, when the date of their wedding anniversary came around, announced to the table, "If your mother and I had stayed married, this would be our forty-eighth anniversary," or forty-ninth, fiftieth, etc., which I usually acknowledged with a nod and a dubious "Huh."

Though we enacted this almost hyperreal family tableau every week, I didn't like my father calling attention to it. I preferred, perhaps as my parents had when I was young, to not identify what was happening. Maybe I was afraid if we named it, it would go away.

Several years passed and then I began flipping through the books my father had brought me. I was ready to learn what it was the man whose cassettes my mother shut herself in her room to listen to was promising; what he offered that Nava and I couldn't.

Reading through Bhagwan's books I tried to put myself in my mother's shoes; would I have been impressed by his lectures? I wondered if I would have been able to see through what from my present vantage point seemed like a heap of strung-together empty words.

But more than the specifics of Bhagwan's teachings, I wanted to know what living on his ashrams had been like so I ordered more books: *My Life in Orange* by Tim Guest, *Stripping the Gurus* by Geoffrey D. Falk, and *The Rajneesh Chronicles* by Win McCormack. I read them when I was alone in the house and could keep my research to myself.

In Pune, where Bhagwan had established a six-acre ashram in a residential neighborhood, my mother became Ma Gyam Shanti, the Indian name her guru gave her. Born Chandra Rajneesh he had changed his own name to Bhagwan, which means God in Sanskrit. I have to wonder where my mother's bullshit detector had gone. To me, anyone who identifies themselves as God is someone I want to stay away from. My mother was from Brooklyn, which should have equipped her with at least a little bit of an edge, but I guess she wasn't cynical enough to question if he was for real. Or, perhaps the appeal of being told how to dress, how to think, and what to do was too intoxicating for her to think critically about who he might actually be, and what he was offering. Maybe being on her own in Seattle had left her depleted and vulnerable enough that she had no resistance left.

When we've spoken about this in recent years, she says that she didn't think of Bhagwan as a god and insists she never gave herself over completely. She remembers there were people on the ashram who wouldn't do anything without his approval but maintains that was not the case for her. She was on a spiritual journey and went there, she says, with an urgency to improve herself; to become a better person and a better mother. She didn't want to suffer or be in pain anymore.

In the mid-to-late 1970s about six thousand sannyasins lived in and around the complex in Pune. As word spread of Bhagwan's teachings, the ashram grew even more crowded with Westerners flocking to be near their spiritual master. Bhagwan lectured every day and sannyasins were tasked with whatever jobs, menial or otherwise, needed doing. Making money while in India wasn't easy for ashram visitors. Some women turned to prostitution, some people sold drugs. I know my mother eventually gave Tarot readings to help pay for the apartment she rented nearby with someone she'd met.

In his book *The Rajneesh Chronicles,* author Win McCormack describes dangerous ashram "therapy groups," some of which resulted in "broken bones, rapes, and mental breakdowns."

Incredibly, given the reports that eventually came out about life in the Pune ashram, my mother doesn't recall any of that in the therapy groups and workshops she participated in. She is positive those things happened in the early 70s, and not when she was there in 1979. It may be that she arrived in Pune after those methods were discontinued, but she also doesn't recall any of the other menacing aspects of the ashram depicted in *Wild Wild Country,* the six-part docuseries that got me to dig deeper into my family's past.

Men were urged to get vasectomies and reportedly about a quarter of them did. Women were encouraged to get sterilized. The object of the game was to unencumber yourself so you could reach enlightenment. If you were unfortunate enough to already have kids, it was best to leave them with someone, like my mother did. If that wasn't an option, then the kids came along to the ashram but didn't spend time with or live with their parents.

Some children did live on the ashram, but by all accounts they weren't looked after much. While their parents participated in meditation sessions and worked on the ashram, the kids stayed in housing together which was vaguely reminiscent of the kibbutz, except they weren't cherished or nurtured in the same way. I don't know what my mother truly felt when she saw kids on the ashram—if she ever missed Nava and me, or felt any kind of tug pulling her home. When I asked her about this, she began to answer but trailed off. My guess is she didn't or if she did, she reassured herself knowing we were safe with our father.

What she did notice when she saw kids on the ashram, she told me, was that they seemed happy and that she wasn't aware that they lived separately from their parents. I can't imagine she didn't notice the way the boys and girls ran around in packs with no supervision or that children of all ages witnessed sannyasins having sex, often out in the open.

In his book *Stripping the Gurus,* author Geoffrey Falk writes that Bhagwan condoned young teenage girls being romantically and sexually matched with much older men. Sometimes he asked couples to have sex in front of him and sometimes he asked women to strip for him. The guru also sought out a dozen larger-breasted women to join a group of select "mediums" for a special, restricted-group for "energy darshans." In these private sessions he was said to "conduct" his energy out into the world for the greater good via these twelve buxom sannyasins. Yikes.

In interviews I've read that some people who grew up on the ashram remember the experience as being a good one, that they were free and could explore and carve out their own lives in Pune, or on Rancho Rajneesh, the Oregon ranch. Others have less fond memories of their time as a young sannyasin. I suppose if I had gone as a child and had been raised amongst Bhagwan's disciples and steeped in his teachings, surrounded by other kids on the loose like me, I'd have grown used it. Maybe I would have liked the blurry boundaries and the absence of parents, the missing family structure. Undoubtedly, I would have become a wholly different person. But it's because of the role Bhagwan played in my life that I fully reject everything he stood for, and what he offered his followers.

And ultimately, it wouldn't have mattered if I had gone to live with my mother on the ashram. I would have lost her anyway.

Worldly

I'd been in second grade at Mount Vernon Elementary school in Newark for a few months and things didn't feel as bad as I'd feared. I had some friends and was doing well in school. Soon after I turned seven, I asked my father about babies and where they came from. Always happy to teach, he grabbed a notepad and pen and sat me down at the dining room table. In a warm but academic way he told me about ovaries, the uterus, and the fallopian tubes. He lived for this kind of professorial exchange and wanted to ensure I felt no shame about my anatomy. I was so comfortable with my father back then, so safe, like he was my best friend and confidant. Spending time with him was like being chosen as part of the inner circle, especially because he was the only male in our new family of six—something I know he loved. He thrived on being the center of attention, especially attention from women.

My father continued casually sketching the female reproductive system while I leaned over to see his diagrams.

"You know when I was a kid," he said, "my parents didn't tell me anything about reproduction. Whatever I knew I learned from my friends. I want you to feel comfortable about asking me questions. You can always bring them to me."

"Okay," I nodded.

He had drawn the ovaries and the uterus and the fallopian tubes but I was still confused about how babies started and why I didn't have one yet. We talked about the vagina and the penis; we talked about hormones and puberty.

"But how can the penis go into a woman's vagina? It's mushy," I said.

Without hesitation, he explained rushing blood, erections, orgasms, and sperm.

I nodded again, mulling it over. Just when we'd gotten past what adult-me sees as the most embarrassing exchange a parent and child could have, I said, "What does an orgasm feel like?"

He paused. "Well," he said tapping his pen on the notepad while he thought about it. "Have you ever had to go to the bathroom really, really bad and then you finally get to go?"

"Definitely!"

"It feels kind of like that," he said, which I still think is a very good way to answer that question.

I was thrilled that I had so much information about being grown up. That week when I was in class, I opened my black composition notebook to re-sketch the breasts, the vagina—clitoris included—the ovaries, the uterus, the penis, and the testicles. I then labeled these parts in my left-handed scrawl. At break I decided to show my teacher.

Mrs. Johnson, a shorthaired woman with medium brown skin and average build, wore a mild expression most of the time, the kind of smile the woman at the movie ticket counter offers you when she gives you your change. I felt pleased with what I remembered from my conversation with my father, though I also had a sense I probably shouldn't have drawn this in class because it was not what we were studying, and because the topic was a private one. But I also wanted to show her that I was more than an average second grader. I wanted to convince her I was mature enough to handle the sex stuff my classmates whispered and giggled about.

"Look," I said, "I drew the parts of the human body."

She scanned the diagrams I held up to her in a pleasant but

noncommittal way. Then she leaned closer to inspect my two-page spread.

"See," I said, "here are the breasts, this is a penis, and this is a vag—"

The set of her mouth didn't change; only the new tilt of her head let me know she had looked at it long enough. "Mm hmm," she said, simultaneously handing me back my book and closing it shut. "You can do that at home."

Because I was very good at following directions, I continued working on my sketches at home.

Janine saw me drawing in my notebook that afternoon and said, "I'm telling on you. You're going to get in trouble."

I was pretty sure that wasn't true. Almost one hundred percent certain. And with that confidence, I said, "No, I won't."

When she told my father, he assured her that my drawings were fine, just as I presumed he would. I now had another reason to be smug around Janine. Here was proof that my relationship with my father was special and separate from how she knew him and another way my family was different from hers—a good thing, in my opinion.

Janine had a friend from middle school named Nicki, who didn't live in the projects with us. She had braces and shoulder-length curly hair, with bangs.

One day at the park, I heard Janine talking to Nicki.

"You should see what she drew in her notebook, all kinds of private parts."

I ignored her. I pumped my legs on the swing to go higher. I loved the wind in my hair. I liked the way the sun sank and rose into view every time I dipped and made it up toward the sky again. I soared past the dirty sandbox I could see in the corner of my eye, past the kids stuck on the ground. I climbed higher than the poking tops of the wrought iron fence that enclosed the park. I was bolder, happier, freer there than anywhere else. Everything about being on the swing was better than the pavement and grown-ups and roaches and noise on the ground below. On the swing it was only me, alone. I got to be away from the people who I otherwise had to listen to and the home I was stuck in.

In the Bush by Musique had just ended and *This is Ladies Night* by Kool and the Gang was now blaring from a boom box below, where teenagers older than Janine and Nicki were clustered.

"I'm serious, ask her what the song is about," Janine told Nicki.

"Okay, okay, I'll do it," Nicki said, a little exasperated with Janine, or maybe embarrassed. "Ronit," she said, leaning on the pole nearest my swing, "what does this song mean?"

Romantic lady, single baby, Sophisticated mama, come on you disco lady, yeah, Stay with me tonight, mama, yeah.

I listened to the lyrics and thought for a moment about how to answer.

If I showed my ability to understand adult stuff, I would impress these older kids, but it was a dubious distinction. Still eager to prove myself as mature as I believed I was, I took the bait. "It's about women going out and looking for men and men looking for women. But not like prostitutes or women of the night."

I kept on pumping high, pretending I had no stake in the game, pretending I didn't care that I had likely impressed Nicki.

"See?" Janine said, shaking her head. "I told you."

Halloween was coming and with my Israeli accent gone I felt almost like a full-fledged American kid now. I wanted to be my all-time favorite superhero, Wonder Woman, and I practiced Lynda Carter's spin; I studied her costume. She entranced me: the beauty of her delicate yet well-formed shoulders, her lean arms, her incredible boots, her gorgeous hair, and blue eyes. And I was fascinated by her tiny waist, perhaps intuiting I would never attain such a measurement myself. Everything about her, from her eyes to her breasts to her legs, was perfect. I could find no flaw. That's what I wanted to be. Smooth and polished and invincible and beautiful. I wanted to know what I had to do to get there, to be that.

The drugstore Wonder Woman costume my father got for me was in a ten-by-twelve-inch package and, besides the mask, came folded up almost flat. I ripped open the clear plastic wrapper and was immediately hit by the pungent smell of vinyl. I unfolded the white rectangle five times and stared at the thin plastic-tablecloth material with a cartoon picture of Wonder Woman's outfit printed on the front. What the hell? I didn't want to wear a stupid tablecloth with a *picture* of Wonder Woman's outfit, I wanted her actual outfit: her golden cuffs, her belt, the bodysuit, her boots. I wanted to become her.

I tried pulling the vinyl onesie on over my clothes but it was too snug so I stripped and put the costume on over just my underwear. The facemask that came with it was cut in the shape of Wonder Woman's hair but really short, in a goofy, hard plastic bob. It, too, was a picture of hair, not the real thing. I didn't know what the adults in charge of making costumes could be thinking or how any kid could fall for this charade. It pained me that this shoddy getup was the closest I could get to becoming the superhero I longed to be. But I was nothing if not committed, so I got the pillowcase I was using for a trick-or-treat bag and met Nava and Janine, who was in charge of watching us, at the door.

I put on the mask and tried to line up the slots for my eyes and the smaller ones for my nostrils as perfectly as I could. But if I got one eye right, the other wasn't aligned. The mask made my face hot and the costume, still not roomy enough for my thicker trunk even though I had only underwear on underneath, strained as I walked. I peered out of my one lined-up eyehole and took halting, very un-Wonder Woman like steps to keep everything in place.

Ten minutes later and three pieces of candy in I reached up to wipe the sweat trickling from my temple when I felt something give near my legs. Air wafted over my thighs and I looked down to see the vinyl onesie torn open at the crotch. There was my light blue underwear. Through my one eyehole I saw Janine staring at me but I refused to look at her. I pulled the two sides of my costume together in my hands, and hobble-walked over to the next apartment door, cursing my bad luck and Janine for being there to witness my humiliation. We tried a few more apartments but no one answered and Janine said we needed to get back. Alone in the bathroom at home, knowing I had failed Halloween and angry at my dumb body for being too big to fit into my costume, I ripped off what was left of it and tossed it into the trash.

~

I decided if I couldn't be perfect, I would try to get special attention for having something wrong with me. Despite my longtime wish for a hospital stay, like I'd read in *Madeline*, it looked like my appendix was fine and wouldn't be coming out anytime soon. Same for my tonsils. I hadn't even ever broken anything—it seemed I was indestructible. At school I read a book called *Sue, The Girl with the Button in her Ear,* about a protagonist who wore a hearing aid. I wanted one too so when the school gave us hearing tests in November, I decided I would purposely try to fail mine by ignoring some of the beeps.

I put on the black headphones with small cushions that cradled each ear, and I responded to the first few beeps by raising my hand on whichever side the beep had sounded. Then the next time I heard a beep I ignored it. I stared at the audiologist as if I'd heard nothing. I did this after several more beeps, giving myself a couple of accurate responses in between. She looked over at me and made a note. I was certain she was going to mark in my record that I had a problem and I couldn't wait for her to call my father and tell him I needed a hearing aid. Finally, I would have something officially wrong with me. A medical condition to set me apart, make me fragile and in need of being taken care of. At minimum, a hearing problem meant doctors, tests, and separate time alone with my father who would have to call my mother and tell her I had a problem. Days passed, then weeks without word. Had I responded to too many beeps? Had they lost my results? The audiologist never called.

I may have gotten the idea that a medical condition was what I needed by watching my father and my Newark family care for Nava through a skin condition. She had broken out in blisters and bumps, fluid-filled and tender, on her palms and fingers. The sandbox at the park is where my father thought she picked up the virus on her hands. She was four and a half and spent more time with our babysitter, Joyce than I did. Plus, she played in the sandbox, which I avoided. With the dirty-looking sand, occasional cigarette butts and candy wrappers and the stray cats that hung around, there was no way I would touch it. My father took Nava to the doctor, but they couldn't figure out what had made her skin break out into these pustules.

With Tracy's help, and with assistance from the big girls when they were home, my father coated Nava's hands in ointments and wrapped them in gauze twice a day to protect her and others, and to help the blisters heal. She didn't have use of her fingers when the bandages were on; she walked around with gauze completely covering her hands and parts of her wrists like boxing gloves, and people who asked about her thought she was a burn victim.

I felt bad for my sister. I knew she was suffering; I heard her whimper with pain and itching, but I kept my distance from her. I knew it was lucky it wasn't me. Now, I wish I had been more generous. After a month of applying ointment to her hands and wrapping them in gauze, the blisters went away and she never contracted them again.

~

I couldn't be perfect, and I couldn't get special attention so the only other option was to make waves. Nava and I were in the bathroom for the few minutes we had it to ourselves in the mornings, between turns by Janine and Sarah, Tracy, and my father. As I was putting toothpaste on my toothbrush, I got some on my finger and accidentally smeared toothpaste in my bangs.

Nava laughed.

"Shut up," I told her.

"Make me," she said and stuck out her tongue.

This infuriated me. "You better shut up or I'll squeeze toothpaste on your face," I said, staring her down.

"Dare you," she said, casually, without a trace of fear.

In that moment I felt the wool of my tights scratch against my legs, the too-tight waistband of my hand-me-down skirt digging into my potbelly. I heard the fast click of Tracy's high heels in the hallway and her goodbye to Sarah and Janine, and realized I was going to have to hurry not to be late for school. My little sister, the only person who looked up to or relied on me at all, was no longer intimidated by me. I officially had no place in this family.

I picked up our tube of Crest and squeezed a line of toothpaste across Nava's cheek. She squealed.

The next thing I heard were my father's pounding footsteps.

He opened the door and hollered, "What's going on in here?"

Nava told him what I had done. He raised his hand and, before I could grasp what was happening, he walloped me with a smack on the bum.

I was stunned. Insulted. But I knew I deserved it. Up until then, I had this idea I was on par with Tracy, above punishment, because my father usually treated me with so much respect. His disciplining me reminded me I was still just a kid and I had to watch myself. I had to play by this family's rules.

Mothership

We got letters from my mother every now and then, in which she alluded vaguely to when she'd come get us, but then later she would move the date again.

One Saturday when she was supposed to call, my father let me skip errands with the family and stay home with Sarah, who was observing Shabbat, the day of rest. I was unable to draw or focus on my book or do anything but wait for my mother to call. I stayed near the phone, twitching ahead of the ring. The morning faded into afternoon and the afternoon ticked by until my father and Tracy and Janine and Nava returned, and we all ate dinner. Afterward, I went back to sit near the phone, and I stayed there for the rest of the night. My father had to walk me to my room when it was time for bed. I made him promise to wake me up if she called after I was asleep. I tried not to shut my eyes, but my body was done for the day; I was worn out and deflated, still hoping my father would get me and I'd hear her voice on the line. I'd been trying to get home but I didn't know where that was anymore. What did it mean if the person I was waiting for to rescue me from this situation I found myself in, living with a family that didn't belong to me, wasn't coming back?

~

In the spring of 1979, Nava's babysitter was still Joyce, the mother of LaTonya, a classmate of mine, who lived in the building. Joyce watched Nava while LaTonya and I were at school and occasionally watched both of us in her apartment after school. Joyce had three children. I never met her husband. Her daughter, Jasmine, was in fourth grade, and her son, Andre, in eighth.

I was at Joyce's one day when Andre came home, and I knew to give him a wide berth as soon as he walked into their apartment. When he saw me on the couch with LaTonya he scowled, and I felt keenly both my little-girlness and my whiteness. He didn't seem to want me there, but neither of us had a choice. In my discomfort and intrigue, I giggled something into LaTonya's ear.

"You know you don't want to be messing with me, girl," Andre said, shooting me a stern look. No one had spoken to me like that before, and I stopped giggling. I watched him across the room, where he sat by the door retying the shoelaces of his brand new bright white sneakers. I was afraid of him but I wanted him to like me. It felt that if he did, I might be safer.

Joyce lightened the mood and asked who wanted to have a MoonPie. I had never heard of them before, but whatever it was sounded magical and possibly delicious. She brought a carton of them out from the kitchen and spread them out, each one in its own plastic wrapper, in front of us. I watched LaTonya open hers and did the same. I tasted the soft crumbly cookie coated in chocolate, the thin bouncy layer of marshmallow inside. The flavor wasn't anything I could identify, a weak taste with just a suggestion of goodness. I didn't love it, but I ate it anyway. I didn't want to call attention to myself and give Andre a reason to notice me again. After that afternoon I managed to stay out of his way.

One day that spring, LaTonya took me into her bedroom to show me a light pink satin dress still with the tags on, laid out on her twin bed. She would wear it for Easter the following Sunday. On top were a crisp white camisole and little white ruffled socks, and on the floor next to the bed were new white patent leather Mary Janes. It was the kind of clothing I had never seen up close before, had never owned.

White dress shoes! Besides a beloved pair of navy-blue clogs I had worn nearly every day in Seattle, I had never owned shoes in colors other than brown or black. Across from LaTonya's bed, up against the wall with two windows, was her sister Jasmine's bed, and it too was draped with a pink satin dress. She also had a pristine pair of white patent leather shoes and socks, but on top of her dress was a new bra, which was amazing to me.

The outfits were brand new and untouched. LaTonya's mother had thought of her and bought these things and placed them on the bed for her like a present. I had never had anyone surprise me this way; even on the kibbutz I picked outfits from bins of communal clothing. The clothes I wore now were what I'd brought from Seattle and occasional hand-me-downs from Janine and Sarah. It hit me in my gut: I understood for the first time that something as ordinary as clothing could become a gift if someone who loved you, who was keeping you in mind, picked it out, and gave it to you.

You can get used to the way things are, the way you live, so you don't have to think about it too much and it doesn't bother you. But after seeing LaTonya's Easter outfit, I wanted new clothes like that; I wanted the surprise. And, although it was not conscious, I wanted the most important part: a mother to think of me. Had I realized what I needed from my mother in that moment, I might have blown apart into tiny pieces, scattered into dust all over Jasmine and LaTonya's bedroom.

~

I was seven-and-a-half when my father told me my mother was returning from India after ten months away. Her mother had breast cancer, and she was coming back to help. In years since, I have wondered more than a few times when she would have returned if my grandmother hadn't gotten sick. I don't know if she planned on returning to India afterward or if she thought she would stay in the States.

I also wonder what feelings my father must have had when he told Nava and me. He probably worried what the news would do to us and he also might have had concern and distrust about who my mother was now, after her travels. She was an unknown quantity for us all.

The night before my mother was due to arrive, I had a hard time sleeping. I fussed over what to wear, picking out my best jeans and best sweater, the white one threaded with silver tinsel.

After school the next day, Joyce was at our apartment watching us for our father, who was at work. I remember being surprised that he wouldn't make arrangements to be there when my mother returned. I couldn't have understood then how much he didn't want to see her.

I wanted to look pretty for my mother, and I wanted her to be happy she was back.

"Joyce?"

"Uh huh?"

"Will you do my hair special?"

"Sure." She smiled and gestured for me to come over. I stood next to where she sat, and she ran the brush through my hair, picking a small tangle out so gently, without pulling.

"How do you want it?" she asked, resting a hand on my shoulder.

"Back on each side please with these clips."

I could barely stand still while she fixed my hair. I was vibrating.

When she was done, I went to Nava, whom I had been kind to all day, and grabbed her face in both my hands and said, "Mommy is almost here!" She held onto my hands.

My smile: I couldn't get rid of it. I couldn't carry a thought through. I couldn't believe she was actually coming back, that I was going to see her.

The doorbell rang. My heart knocked in my chest.

Joyce went to the door. I heard the twisting sounds of the first and then the second lock clicking open. The clanking of small links as Joyce slid the door chain back on its runner.

Finally, I could let out the breath I'd been holding. The one that I belonged to was back.

The door groaned open, echoing in the apartment hallway. My mother's body in its billowy, sunset-color clothing filled the doorframe. My mother. Tall, beautiful, and radiating a kind of calm. But something in her eyes wasn't how I pictured it. I missed the moment when she seemed as happy to see me as I was to see her.

She had big hair and a nose ring and she jingled when she walked in. She was wearing an anklet of small, bright, dangling silver bells that tinkled with each step and around her neck I saw she still had on her black mala with the photo of Bhagwan's face hanging at its end. Still, I went to her and I hugged her, the beads of her necklace wedged between us, marking our separation, a reminder of how she was no longer mine.

So Long, Suckers

My mother had returned, but not to bring us with her to Seattle to live together as she had once promised. She explained that she wasn't in a position to take us yet. She was in Brooklyn caring for Grandma Lina, who was sick with breast cancer, and we would begin to visit the two of them every other weekend once she got herself settled. But the school year was starting and, for the second time in as many years, my father made a last-minute decision about our future.

In the summer of 1980 my father, Nava, and I moved out of Ivy Hill.

My last memorable interaction with Tracy was when I was almost eight. I had met her, Sarah, Janine, and my father in the city on a Sunday, after sleeping over at my grandmother Lina's.

The night before, my mother had taken Nava and me to a Chinese restaurant for dinner and then let us pick out treats like Mint Milanos, Ruffles Sour Cream and Onion potato chips, and Haagen-Dazs Vanilla Swiss Almond ice cream at the corner store before we headed back to my grandma's. After we said hi to Grandma Lina, who was home from cancer surgery, we flopped in front of the TV to watch *The Love Boat* and *Fantasy Island*. The next morning my mother set out a gorgeous homemade breakfast like she did every weekend she had us, complete with fried eggs, bagels, lox, and fruit. I wasn't used to so much freshly prepared food in the morning. Cereal was what we had for breakfast with my father, because he always had to go to work.

We needed to get back into Manhattan early that afternoon for an event at my father's nonprofit, but before we left Brooklyn to meet him and Tracy and the girls, I asked my mother to do my hair up for me. I usually wore my hair down but I wanted to look special for the day. I wanted to return to my temporary family transformed now that my mother was back to take care of me.

Except for that one time when my babysitter Joyce had styled me, I wasn't used to having anyone but me work with my hair and it was a new feeling to have this part of my body handled by my mother, to give myself over to her as she brushed it away from my face. I liked the sensation of her hands sweeping all of my hair up, trusting her as she smoothed it around my head, and then tucked it neatly up into a bun. When I checked myself in the mirror, I saw she had made me look exactly right. And, just as I had asked, she left my bangs down, so they covered my forehead the way I liked.

I didn't want to say goodbye to her when we got to the lobby where my father and Tracy and the girls were waiting—leaving her when Sunday afternoon came around was hard each time—but my perfect hair softened the blow. I was ready to make a grand entrance. Nava and I hugged her goodbye and she left.

"Hey, kid," my father said and hugged me.

I held my head and shoulders more upright. I felt beautiful and grown up, and hoped Tracy, Janine, and Sarah would take note that my mother and I were connected, that this is what I looked like when she took care of me. I think I probably stared back at them as if from a perch.

After they'd greeted Nava and me there was conversation. I heard Tracy say something about "too mature," and she told Sarah and Janine to redo my hair. She handed Sarah a comb from her purse.

"I don't want to take it out," I said, protecting the bun with my hand.

"It will be better this way," Tracy said, "better for your age."

I looked to my father but he wasn't going to get involved.

Janine began to take out the bobby pins from my hair and the bun loosened. I stood there while she worked, my teeth clenched, my eyes boring straight ahead of me. A scene came to mind, where Cinderella's stepsisters rip off the dress she sewed herself so she could go to the ball. In reality, I sensed Janine's reluctance in following her mother's directions, but Cinderella is who I felt like with my pseudo-stepsister sliding out bobby pin after bobby pin until my hair came spilling down around my face. I didn't know why they thought it was all right for them to do this, or why my father wasn't making them stop. It's possible my father had no idea that what looked like a simple hairdo change felt to me like a wrecking ball slamming into a building.

Sarah brought over the comb Tracy gave her, and Janine smoothed my hair. I thought if I couldn't keep my bun, I could live with my hair down. But then Tracy came over and gathered up the front part of my hair, including my bangs, and Janine pulled them back taut. She clipped them with a barrette so I had nothing covering my forehead. It was my least favorite way of wearing my hair, with my full cheeks making me look like a preschooler. I dagger-eyed Tracy when I could manage it. I could not forgive her for forcing me to do what she wanted, for not letting me keep part of my mother with me that day.

In the family photograph we took of the six of us at the event just afterward, I stare back at the camera, incensed and certain that Tracy is evil. I would have gotten angry if anyone took me in hand and altered the way I had styled my own hair, but because my mother had done so, it was far worse.

I wish I had stuck up for myself then, but I think I was already pretty tired of hoping adults would understand what I needed. I wanted to feel good in my own skin for once, not like I needed fixing. It's also clear to me, looking back now, that I was able to summon far more anger for Tracy over a hairstyle than toward my mother for leaving. But that, I think, is the nature of filial love. Parents can get away with so much with their children. And it was safer to push Tracy away than my own mother.

In any case, when we did move away from Tracy, Sarah, Janine, and Ivy Hill a few weeks later, I could allow myself to think: *So long, suckers, I knew I'd get out.*

New Digs

I was sitting with the rest of my third-grade class on the library rug fussing with my tights, which, as usual, were not quite long enough for my legs, when Mrs. Nelson, the librarian at my brand-new school in Flushing, Queens opened *Are You My Mother?* My head snapped up; I had heard this book before. Once she began reading it and showing us the illustrations, I felt like I was visiting a long-forgotten place.

The book about a baby bird who falls out of his nest and goes searching for his mother was an echo of a time and part of my life I hadn't thought of in years; now I remembered it in my bones. My mother and father had read the book to me and Nava when we still lived in Seattle together, when we cuddled at bedtime before they separated.

I kept my body still, practically holding my breath so I wouldn't miss a word. I panicked when the baby bird put himself in graver and graver danger on his quest to find his mother. I was afraid for him and I knew—just as my father had been reminding Nava and me anytime we took the subway with him, or walked in a crowded space—that if you got lost you should stay in one place so your parent could find you. I didn't understand why the baby bird kept moving farther away from where he had dropped from his nest—how dumb could you be? At the same time, a part of me understood deeply why he felt it was his job to go out, find his mother, and bring her back home.

~

My father chose to move us to Flushing in part because his father, now married to his second wife, had an apartment there. Grandpa Sammy was tall with a full head of curly hair like my father. He had been a typesetter and had left my grandmother, my father, and his sister, my Aunt Ellen, when my father was in high school so he could marry the woman he was having an affair with. My father told me that he had never felt more bereft than when his father moved out of the apartment.

When my kids were fourteen and twelve, he and I were standing in my kitchen while I stirred a pot of marinara sauce for Shabbat dinner, and I asked him about his parents' divorce.

"I was inconsolable, a mess," he said. "The day my father moved out was the worst day of my life. I swore I wouldn't allow myself to cry again about anything unless it was as serious and painful as that." He took a sip of water. "And I never did."

"What about when you got divorced yourself and moved away from me and Nava?" I asked, breaking eye contact to look at the pot of sauce, worried that he wouldn't remember the afternoon he said goodbye to us in Seattle when I was five, which I count as one of the most painful of my childhood.

"Are you kidding? That was the next time I cried like that. It was a terrible day, terrible."

"It was," I said, stirring. "It really was."

So many tears in this family, so many people leaving one another. It's not lost on me that though I'm a grown up I still needed to hear that I was important enough to my father that separating from me made him cry. That's one of the most damaging legacies of leaving children: the doubt they carry that they're good enough to stick around for. I know I've struggled with that my whole life.

Turned out our moving to Flushing didn't matter that much to Grandpa Sammy and his wife. We saw them a handful of times before they packed it in and relocated to Florida.

Flushing was an inexpensive neighborhood, so my father was able to find us a three-bedroom, two-bathroom apartment in a building called The Kissena, named for our street. Our building was only eight blocks away from the 7 train, the subway that took him into the city for work.

Compared with Ivy Hill, our new building was sprawling and had a doorman. I hadn't seen a lot of apartment building lobbies so didn't have much to compare it to. To me the lobby looked fancy, with its columns and white, shiny floors inlaid with silver flecks, each large tile separated from the next by slim bands of silver, like ribbon on square gift-wrapped presents. The Kissena had two wings and we lived in the one to the left of the lobby, past a room full of mailboxes and a long hallway.

The individual floors of the building with gray walls and burgundy carpeting were poorly lit. When the elevator arrived on our floor, we turned right and walked down the hall past an apartment rented by a small British woman named Elizabeth, who lived next to the incinerator room. The warm air in the corridor was stuffy, smelling of garbage and old smoke. Our unit was at the end. Apartment 333—and three was my favorite number. It was auspicious. And three times three equaled nine, which was the number of September, my birth month. Three was also the number of people in my family. I loved the coincidence of it—how three had now appeared all over my life, like magic.

Our first weekend in the new place, Nava and I skipped down Kissena Boulevard alongside my father, chattering about what kind of sofa we'd get, what color rug. This was our new beginning, our fresh start with our father, the parent who wanted us. We passed Key Food, the bank, the Friendly Donuts coffee shop displaying its sugared, sprinkled, and frosted goodness in the window, and a hardware store. Above, just a little further down the block, was an overpass where the Long Island Railroad tracks crossed Kissena Boulevard. Flushing was the last stop for the 7 and for the LIRR. "Under the bridge," which is what Nava and I called the dim space beneath the overpass, were stalls with Chinese slippers, jelly shoes, bangles, plastic toys, bandanas, belts, and lace headscarves that the vendors sold for cheap. Nava and I were transfixed. Our father said we could come back another time, and we moved on.

We passed Barone's Pizza, Modell's Sporting Goods, Alexander's Department Store, The Wiz music shop, and a Burger King, and then the furniture stores started cropping up. We only went into the ones with sales. Near the end of the series of shops, I stopped at a display window and pointed out the queen bed, draped in a white faux-fur bedspread stacked with fluffy animal-print pillows against a mirrored headboard. A slender floor lamp placed to the bed's right side rose up tall, past the headboard, and swooped over the bedspread like a long, silver-necked bird, casting its glow over the furry cover. I stared at it through the window.

To me the bed was elegant and sophisticated. Woman-y. I didn't want to be a chunky, chubby-cheeked kid living in an ugly city any longer than I had to. I couldn't wait to break out of this wrapper so I could claim what was mine: the satiny blush-colored world of the models in L'Oreal commercials, the Enjoli perfume ads. I wanted to grow up as soon as I could and shed this little girlness and, when I did, I'd be a silky, sensual, glamorous woman. This kind of woman. Certainly, the woman I would become had to be better than who I was now.

The living room furniture we went to see that day beckoned "Dream Home," "Modern," "Roach-Free," and yet the couch my father settled on was a more masculine bristly tweed and featured repeating stripes in five alternating shades of brown. Only one stripe was not scratchy and woolen: the light beige section, which was more like velvet than the coarse fabric of the rest of the stripes. When I sat on the couch at home, I would find this stripe and run my hands across it to feel the plush fabric against my fingertips. It was like a reassurance that there was part of the sofa that could redeem it, that was pretty and fresh and different from the rest of the apartment.

I had high hopes for a modern new living room in mauve or rose, even shades of blue, but, alas, everything else my father bought was also in brown and toffee-toned neutrals, the epitome of 80s furniture. He picked out a beige armchair for himself. Nava and I were not allowed in his "Dad" chair, where he would rest and watch TV and sip his one nightly glass of scotch, though we sometimes spun in it when he wasn't home.

We got a low wood coffee table, two end tables, a few lamps, and—voila—we were moved in. Our father knew how important a pretty room was to Nava and me so he let us get matching quilted, nylon bedspreads in yellow chiffon, printed with white flowers and trimmed with ruffles. When we made our beds, I inserted our new pillows into the matching pillow shams and set them at the headboard. I arranged a few stuffed animals and one of the small decorative throw pillows my father had allowed each of us to get, and I looked around our new room. I took in the chalk-white paint, the bracketed shelves and metal shelf standards my father had installed that ran up the top half of the wall with their empty slots for future brackets, my dark brown pressboard desk near the windows fitted with child safety bars, and the fire escape outside. I think I believed that once our new bedspreads were on the beds, our room would become the girlhood, TV-family bedroom of my dreams. But though the three of us tried, the apartment remained a bit dingy.

~

We were all moved in and summer break was almost over. My father took Nava and me shopping for school supplies and clothes to add to our hand-me-downs. On the Wednesday after Labor Day I wore my crisp first-day-of-school white blouse, and my hair pinned up in a purple barrette on either side with my bangs down and the three of us walked to P.S. 20. I found my place in line on the playground where Mrs. Kaplan's third grade class was meeting and said goodbye to my father. I didn't cry this time.

An ocean of new faces, one after the next, bobbed into view as I tried to get my bearings. I looked at my new classmates, most of whom seemed to know each other, and I adjusted my backpack. Many of these kids' parents, I would discover, were from Korea, China, Japan, Greece, India, Pakistan, Brazil, Venezuela, and places I hadn't ever heard of. It wasn't until I had children of my own that I realized that kids usually travel with many of the same classmates throughout their elementary years. Most don't move from school to school as often as I had, meeting new people and leaving them over and over again.

Mrs. Kaplan arrived and checked to make sure we were all in the right line, and I followed the trail of her Ombre Rose perfume, the scent of tea-steeped roses she would wear every day, into the building to my new classroom. I was dazzled by her. Tall, with fair skin and black shiny hair, Mrs. Kaplan was in her early fifties and always wore red lipstick. She favored scarves with her floral blouses and pants or skirts, her heels were not too high but were still feminine, and her blue eyes twinkled both when she talked and when she listened to our answers. Twenty-nine kids were in our class, and she always seemed ready to engage with us. When she wrote on the board, I was mesmerized by the tapping sound of her chalk and by how when she was moving fast her shoulder-length black hair bounced at the ends, where she must have set it in curlers. Sometimes the chalk dust collected on the heel of her right hand as she wrote, and I watched to see if she would catch it before it rubbed off on her clothes. I didn't want her to get smudged.

To me, Mrs. Kaplan was exactly what a teacher, a mother, a grown woman should be and I fell for her hard. Perhaps I imprinted on her because she was the only female figure in my life, or perhaps, I intuited that she liked me. I wanted to make her happy and I did exactly what was expected of me. It never occurred to me not to do my best for her. I sat obediently at my desk, my mouth closed, and hung onto every word. I wanted her to like me as much as I liked her and when she asked the class questions, I almost always raised my hand. In a lucky turn of events, she traveled up to fourth grade with my class the next year, allowing me to have her as my teacher two years in a row.

Sometimes on days my father could walk me to school, he and Mrs.

Kaplan talked in the schoolyard before class. After one of these conversations, he told my sister and me that he was going to change our route to school. Mrs. Kaplan didn't think the way we were going was good for Nava and me. She said the six blocks my father had told us to take were not well-populated enough. She recommended a parallel street two blocks east of Franklin where we could walk more safely.

Flushing was my new home and my classmates felt like my new family. We came from all kinds of experiences, our parents from diverse countries, but in Mrs. Kaplan's class each of us played a part. I looked forward to getting to class, sitting at my wooden desk, having order to my day. I looked at my classmates around the room with a kind of unconditional love, almost as if I was the matriarch—the same approach I'd had on the kibbutz with the children in the younger groups—and assigned each of them roles: the class clown, the smart kid, the cute boy, the sweet girl. I didn't know what my own role was exactly, but I wanted to see these kids every day.

The next year, when many of them wound up in my fourth grade class, I asked my father and Nava to clear out of the kitchen and I spent a weekend baking all thirty-two of them a jumbo homemade pretzel rolled into the shape of the first letter of each of their names. My inspiration was the pretzel vendors in the city but I didn't know anything about baking, nor did I have a pretzel recipe. I mixed pound after pound of white flour with water and some salt into a beige-grey paste that I rolled out, adding even more flour to try to unstick it from the table and rolling pin. The mixture coated my hands and clung to every surface I touched, including the class list of names I'd written to work off of.

The kitchen table, counters, and cabinets were smeared with my thin, stretchy concoction and it was hardening fast. I sprinkled more salt over the top of each finished letter and put batch after batch in the oven, waiting for the dough to transform into what I had envisioned. I couldn't understand why my pretzels didn't turn golden when they baked, why they didn't rise, why the flour and water I shaped became rigid as cement, instead of soft like the pretzels in the hot dog stands, or light or crunchy like the ones in the grocery stores, or why they tasted only like flour. But I still brought them in. Giving them to my classmates was more important to me than whether or not they were perfect. Mrs. Kaplan allowed me to pass my letters out after recess and my classmates inspected their baggies and said thank you, their gratefulness turning to surprise and then confusion as they tried to bite into, then gnaw off pieces of their petrified letters.

I loved lunchtime at the cafeteria—Jamaican beef patties, Sloppy Joes, fish sticks, overcooked green beans. I ate whatever they served, happy to have food cooked for me. I didn't bring a bagged lunch since it was much easier for my father to pay the cafeteria for food, but I was intrigued by the homemade lunches my friends' mothers sent them to school with.

What was it like having someone pack a meal up for you? Sitting with my friends, I eyed the contents of their paper bags, their neat lunchboxes covered with superheroes and TV characters. This was another thing I pined for. I wanted a lunchbox—any lunchbox—so much, I'd make myself feel better when I happened to see one that didn't appeal to me. I'd convince myself it was okay I didn't have *that* one; I didn't need the Hardy Boys or Spiderman, I didn't care about Scooby Doo—the show was weird. I thought Scooby's and Shaggy's scraggly chin scruff was gross. I hated the way Scooby talked; the way he pronounced R as W sounded too much like a slobbery preschool boy.

I didn't like Strawberry Shortcake or Holly Hobby either. There was something too small and precious, too pastel about them. I was after power and primary colors in a lunchbox. The ones I actually wanted for myself were harder to ignore—Wonder Woman of course, or the Bionic Woman, even the Wonder Twins. And the matching thermoses killed me. I especially liked the kind of lunchboxes made of tin with the characters in raised relief. If you ran your fingers over it you could make out the shape, even with your eyes closed. Mainly, though, I pined for the predictability and preparedness of a lunchbox—a little suitcase with what nourished you packed inside.

Around that time, the mother of one of my classmates asked me about my family and I told her my parents were divorced. "Oh, I'm so sorry," she said with a small gasp.

"Why?" I responded as defensively as I could allow myself to sound without disrespecting a grown up. "It's no big deal."

But she searched my face in a way that I resented. To me it felt like pity, like she saw something serious and sad about me and the way I was growing up. I didn't have room to hold onto those kinds of feelings; I couldn't afford them. Besides, I never thought about divorce as being that different or unusual because in my view, everyone got divorced. My parents, my father's parents, my mother's parents, even Uncle Bobby. Divorce seemed to be a given if people made the mistake of getting married. It's still amazing to me that two people can meet and create a life together that they would be able to commit to indefinitely. For me the problem wasn't divorce, it was not living with my mother.

~

There's a photo of my father, my sister, and me from that time in Flushing where we're walking south on Kissena Boulevard together. The photographer, maybe a stranger on the street whom my father had asked, or maybe a girlfriend of my father's, has snapped us in a moment where I am looking up at my father and he has his hand on my forehead, almost like he wants me to look at the camera. Nava is standing next to me and all around us the sky is blue; you can see we're squinting a little bit in the sunshine. Forsythia is in bloom on the hedges behind us and Nava and I are wearing clothes that fit well, and we look well-groomed. Our hair is shiny and smooth-looking and I am still little enough to be cute. It seems like we're having a good time.

We were in the beginning of this section of our life, just a few months into living by ourselves with our father. I feel grateful that at least for a little while, I was able to have some uncomplicated time with him. Nava and I were fortunate because we had a dad who wanted to teach us things and give us confidence in ourselves, who encouraged us to express our opinions and stand up for what we felt was right. He was ready to take us on and try to make our lives as perfect as any father could, as if the three of us were rocking gently in a little boat, sailing off together on safe storybook seas for an exciting new land. He was up for the adventure and at this point that's what our life was.

My father never talked about this with me, but he must have felt how so far, the version of the life he'd dreamed of was not coming true. He was divorced, a single father of two, and back in New York again, far away from his pioneering life in Israel. I wonder how much he allowed himself to feel disappointment or sadness with the outcomes of the choices he'd made.

Miss Piggy

For a while our mother came out to Flushing on the 7 train every other Friday, picked us up at the apartment, and took us to Sheepshead Bay, where Grandma Lina was still battling breast cancer. Carrying bags packed with what we needed for the weekend, the three of us walked to the subway on Main Street to get the 7 into the city. Nava and I were usually chatty on the way down, excited to have the weekend spread before us. I was grateful to be able to get away from my Flushing life, to have a taste even for just two days in a row of living with my mother.

Mom. With her makeup and clothes and the musk and jasmine notes of her Jovan perfume. She led the way through the streets, up tall and away from me, with her separate life and her secrets and private thoughts and the things that went on in her head I could never know. When I was grown and living in the city after I graduated college, I'd often remember how my mother was in those days: 80s jumpsuits, moussed hair, and burgundy lipstick; the way she walked with purpose everywhere we went. At eight years old I matched her gait as best I could and knew I'd grow up to be a woman who knew her way around the city just like her.

Seeing her was like a wish come true every weekend—even going to McDonald's was special because I was with her again. Even so, I was never completely at ease. I had too much at stake hoping our time together would go well. I wonder now if I thought that each time we were together was a sort of trial that could determine whether I'd get to live with her again.

When Nava and I saw her on those weekends, we usually had a fairly easy way of being together and I didn't worry too much. But if she seemed distant or displeased, I tried to tread carefully. It was important not to annoy her. When she looked preoccupied, I interpreted that as her not wanting to be with me. It was especially hard if I needed something from her, even if it was just to double check a memory that I had and wanted to make sure she also remembered.

We were climbing up the back steps of Grandma Lina's house the fall I was eight, the late afternoon sun warming the bricks. Nava and I were waiting for my mother to get her keys out of her purse.

"Mom, you know what Mrs. Kaplan told us?" I asked.

"Can you move away from the lock so I can get in there?"

"I'm sorry," I said and stepped to the side.

"You don't have to say, 'I'm sorry', Ronit." She searched for the right key on her ring.

"Okay." And then like a burp I couldn't control, it popped out: "I'm sorry." I often dropped "I'm sorry" into the middle or at the end of my sentences around her. It was like a magic spell; one I think I believed would keep me in her good graces. But she didn't like it when I apologized.

She looked up at me, annoyed. "Don't say I'm sorry."

"Okay," I said. I smiled and began again. "So, anyway, Mrs. Kaplan told us that if you shake heavy cream hard enough for a long enough time it turns into butter."

My mother had the door open and gathered up a grocery bag. "Nava, come on, come inside," she said.

"Have you ever made cream into butter?" I asked her. "Mom, have you ever made cream into butter?"

"I heard you."

"Oh, sorry." I did it again.

She said I shouldn't say it, but I couldn't tell what she was thinking. Her silence, her ruminations, felt threatening. Was she happy with who I was? Did she like me? What was the trick? What did I have to do to make her want to be with me as much as I wanted to be with her?

~

Even though Grandma Lina was sick, I liked those Brooklyn visits. The house was clean and it had no cockroaches. It smelled like the life that had been lived there, not like old lady or illness. It was a real house; people I was related to had grown up there, and I was allowed to be there and explore. I could treat it like it was mine.

I'd stayed in Grandma Lina's with my mother and Nava the summer of 1976 when we'd first come back from Israel, before we joined my father in Seattle when he was starting at the University of Washington. My first American memory was from that trip: me and my cousin Kurt, who was a few weeks younger, splashing and wading in a blow-up pool under a brilliant blue sky in my grandmother's driveway. I remember the steaming scent of bricks and pavement in the hot July air, water from an emerald-green hose gurgling and glinting in the bright sunlight. The pool was fresh out of the package from Woolworth's, and the vinyl smell was sharp, but I liked it. It kept Kurt and me safe and contained while my mother and Grandmother Lina looked on from their lawn chairs nearby.

Sometimes that summer my mother's sister, Aunt Gloria, took us for rides in her red Dodge Dart Swinger which smelled like new car and Doublemint gum. She had long movie-star hair, wore makeup, and unlike my mother who had somehow avoided it, spoke with a classic Brooklyn accent, chewing on her vowels and dropping her Rs. I knew how much Aunt Gloria got a kick out of me and I loved spending time with her. She introduced me to onion rings, liked to give me toy jewelry and makeup to play with, and always called me darling. My uncle Bobby had red hair and a Brooklyn accent as spectacular as Aunt Gloria's, a good sense of humor, and also a mean streak. He was the oldest and Grandma Lina had treated him as poorly as she'd treated my mother. He was tough with his four kids and knew how to make fun of people where it hurt.

Sheepshead Bay had a spoiled seawater smell at low tide and was named for the Sheepshead fish, which no longer swam in its waters. It was a middle-class neighborhood that had long been an enclave of Jewish refugees from New York's tenement slums and the Soviet Bloc.

Grandma Lina's house was made of brick like so many of the other homes in Sheepshead Bay. Thick wrought-iron bars painted black sprung up from either side of steps that led up to her front porch, enclosed by even more wrought iron. On her stairway, the fourth and fifth bars twisted and swirled until they met in the middle and bloomed into an iron flower. When I was four years old and there for the summer just after leaving Israel, and still now, I liked to run my fingers along the iron, feel the metal's coarse grain, the fine edges on those frozen, tapered petals. Then, if I pressed harder, the sting of their tiny points. I dared myself to see how dangerous they could be, to see how much I could take. When I looked at it, I couldn't decide if I liked that something so powerful had been tamed and sculpted to resemble something pretty, or if I didn't like it because, no matter how ornate the iron was, it couldn't compare to the natural beauty of a real blossom. To me the fake flower was ominous in a way, emulating something that had softness and fragrance with something lifeless and dark. But I knew that a real blossom there made no sense. Eventually its delicate, soft beauty would grow limp and die; at least the hard and dead replica would always stay the same. I liked that it would last.

Hanging over Grandma Lina's porch was a ridged aluminum awning, which, like so many in Sheepshead Bay, was an unnatural shade of green, practically the only burst of color breaking up the endless concrete of Brooklyn. During storms I'd thrill to hear raindrops hitting the corrugated aluminum in hollow pings, then running off the sloping metal with a shimmying rattle.

Very little inside her house was real. Bulbous wax grapes shone on green plastic stems in her crystal bowl of fake fruit. Transparent industrial-strength plastic enclosed every inch of her white-and-brown-floral-velvet sofas and a vinyl carpet runner crossed the length of her living room.

Even though I didn't understand it at the time, I could feel the tension between my mother and my grandmother. A vain woman who dyed her hair blond and then bright red from year to year and relished the idea of being glamorous, my grandmother never told my mother she loved her. She called her names, made fun of her in front of relatives, and shamed her about her appearance and size, even putting her on diet pills when she turned thirteen.

As a teenager, my mother had spent as much time away from home babysitting and at friends' houses as she could to avoid my grandmother and the endless chores she assigned her. Her friends, who were also afraid of Grandma Lina, became the family who seemed to understand who she was. My mother learned early that the only way she could emotionally survive was to leave home and join forces with others.

Grandma Lina was softer with me and Nava. My mother recalls her being genuinely happy to have us there; she brightened up when we were visiting in a way she never did for my mother. She and Grandpa Frank had divorced many years earlier. He was a patient, balding man with light stubble on his face and lids that hung low over his wet, round eyes. He was a chauffeur who bet on horses and played the lottery every day of his adult life. He promised his three children and eventually six grandchildren that when he won, he would be able to take care of us, anything we needed, and for years I got butterflies inside at the notion. But he never won much, at least not enough to change his life or ours. He smoked cigars, big fat ones. To me the tightly packed shredded leaves smelled like dried fruit when he first unwrapped them and toasty when they were lit and burning. A cloud of pungent, ashy air surrounded him wherever he went, and I looked forward to the smell; I liked that it was the same every time.

During that summer I spent in Sheepshead Bay when I was four, Grandpa Frank treated me to my first ever slice of New York-style pizza in Brooklyn. We sat next to each other on shiny red spinning stools at a high Formica counter. Him puffing on his cigar, me negotiating the bubbles in my small plastic cup of Coke that popped and tickled my nose as I drank. I felt calm next to him in a way I hadn't felt with anybody else since I'd gotten to the States. He was steady and slow and didn't talk much, but he didn't seem lost or unpredictable. He behaved like grown-ups were supposed to.

Now, four years later, I didn't see Grandpa Frank much on the weekends I visited my mother. Grandma Lina lay in her hospital daybed in the living room but I tried not to linger whenever I passed her bloated body. It was hard to look at her. All but the finest cob-webby wisps of her hair were gone, and her arms were huge and inflated, swollen from the cancer treatment that had destroyed her lymph nodes. But Grandma Lina, sick and stuck in that bed, still managed to stop me as I tried to flit by unnoticed.

With a glimmer in her drowsy morphine eyes, she liked to ask me if I was the tallest in my class and I was proud to tell her I was even taller than the tallest boy.

One of the last times we talked she asked, "Which grandmother makes the best chopped liver, me or the other one?"

I froze. I could sense I could mess this up, and I watched her scrutinizing me. I knew there was a right answer and a wrong answer and when I thought I had it, I replied in the most casual way I could, "They're both good."

She smiled, but I could tell she didn't quite buy it.

I studied her face only long enough to make sure I was free to go.

As soon as she began lowering herself back down to her pillows, I moved past her and up the stairs to the makeup vanity in her bedroom so I could transform myself. The best part of her house, besides being there with my mother, was playing with Grandma Lina's old makeup and jewelry and clothing. I don't know what it was like for her to watch a granddaughter she barely knew hurry past, bursting up the steps to the bedroom she herself would never see again, hearing me open and shut her dresser drawers and cabinets.

The pop-up trundle bed where I'd fallen and damaged my two baby teeth was still there. I hadn't thought about my silver caps since my permanent teeth had come in. The vanity held all of Grandma Lina's makeup from when she used to wear it, and I rifled through the drawers pulling out tubes and compacts. I opened waxy lipsticks in orange-reds and pinks, so old they smelled like melting crayons, but I didn't mind. I pulled the lipstick across my mouth, pressing my lips together to blend the color like I had seen Aunt Gloria do. I brushed opalescent green eye shadow on my lids and added more and then more until color reached my eyebrows. I dabbed perfumes from almost-empty bottles on my neck, turned my head to the left and right, and admired myself from the corner of my eye. I put on an old dress and my grandmother's strappy silver heels and clopped back down the stairs in sparkling grandeur to show off my artistry to my mother— and, because I couldn't escape her watchful eyes, to the drowsy sentinel at the bottom of the steps whose bedroom I had pillaged. She seemed amused by my attempt at elegance.

Almost a year after my mother's return, my grandmother died. Nava and I missed school and went out to Brooklyn for her funeral, the first I'd ever been to. After the burial, adults I'd never met visited, sitting on the plastic-covered sofa with plates of Jewish-style food on their laps: chopped liver, kosher pickles, noodle kugel, sliced roast beef, rye and pumpernickel bread, rugelach, and buttery bakery cookies dotted with sprinkles.

It had been a while since we'd seen Aunt Gloria or Uncle Bobby who was now divorced and his four kids. I knew he had a temper but I wasn't afraid of him, I was more wary because occasionally when he joked, it was at my expense. I was heavier and taller than my four very slim cousins, with the double chin and full cheeks I'd have until high school. I also had a potbelly and an upturned nose which is probably why he called me Miss Piggy.

Though many months went by between visits when we cousins saw each other, we played together like no time had passed, moving like a unit. But the day of the funeral when we began a game or started laughing, I tried to contain the jubilation. I was the oldest of us six and felt I was responsible for our collective behavior. I knew the day was sad; the adults were sad.

When my youngest cousin, who was not yet four, delicate and milky-fair in her white dress with pink sash and white tights, wanted to use the restroom, I offered to take her upstairs. We passed adults milling around in the living room and climbed the stairs together at a measured pace. I knew we were visible from the living room through the stair railing and I wanted to be seen as the good cousin, the caretaker, the one who would look out for her. I waited as somberly as I could outside the bathroom—the face, I hoped, of maturity and responsibility, reflecting the seriousness of the occasion. How could you pee or visit the bathroom at all in any kind of dignified way, I wondered? I held it most of the day.

On the way back downstairs, I took my cousin's hand. When she asked me a question, I bent over her a little more preciously than I would normally, because I knew chances were good the relatives and guests below would be watching us come back down.

We were halfway down the steps when the sole of my Mary Jane skidded across the carpet and my right foot slipped out from under me. Before I could stop it, my leg buckled and I fell backward, still holding my cousin's hand. Down I went, bringing her with me. Tangled up together, we slid past the last five steps, until we hit the landing and lay crumpled at the bottom, still holding hands.

Everything stopped. The faces in the living room stared. When the surprise of seeing two girls in frilly dresses rolling down the stairs had subsided, my grandmother's neighbor came over to ask if we were okay. I truly wanted to die.

My cousin was fine, just shaken up. As for me, to my disappointment, nothing on me was bleeding or broken. At least if I had gotten hurt my injury would have overshadowed my fall; people would worry over me and take me seriously. But this, this was proof I was a clod. An utter embarrassment at my grandmother's funeral. I had both disrupted those in mourning and almost broken my littlest cousin's neck. Tripping in front of dozens of people, I decided, was what I deserved, a comeuppance for wanting to be graceful and mature instead of the klutz I actually was.

When I had helped my cousin up and pulled my dress back down, still cursing my luck that I wasn't injured, I brought her over to the sofa where Uncle Bobby, her father, was talking to a relative. She sat next to me; her father sat on the other side of her. A few of the funeral guests looked our way and I leaned into the plastic-covered back of the sofa and tucked myself as far back as I could, hoping to make myself invisible.

People passed in front of us and my uncle was talking with my cousin. The room started to return to its original proportions and I could breathe again. I smoothed out the hem of my dress, pulled at the sleeves to adjust the elastic around my wrists and began to shake off what had happened. Then I saw it. The twinkle in my uncle's eye. He was turned toward me and before he could speak, his eyes began to brim. Then they began to water, and I knew. I was too late to get away.

"You two," he wheeze-laughed, "coming down the steps…." He paused, trying to catch his breath between cackles, "You looked like a Miss Piggy snowball."

~

After my grandmother died, my mother got a desk job at a communications company in the city but went on living in the Sheepshead Bay house. My sister and I spent our weekends with her and I slipped into the routine gratefully. Every Friday night, right off the subway, we would stop at the neighborhood convenience store to stock up on provisions we needed to get through the weekend: the usual treats plus bagels and cream cheese, potato chips, and Entenmann's amaretto cheesecake, treats we never got with my father. The three of us would then sit in front of the TV and I would eat until I was stuffed.

Mornings, I woke to sunlight streaming through the bedroom and the smell of my mother's coffee brewing. She fried up eggs for Nava and me and cut up cantaloupe; she poured Tropicana orange juice and buttered our toast. At night I'd sink into my mother's childhood sheets and breathe in the sweet, stale scent of well-used linens, burrowing deeper into the just-right mattress, into bedding worn smooth from so many years of use, dotted with faded flowers and leaves and patterns we didn't have in Flushing.

I was merely visiting an adopted town, an adopted room, lying in someone else's childhood bed. I didn't have a personal history in this house, only a sense of the people and stories that had lived in these rooms, but I wanted it for my own. As the weekends accrued, I gradually began to feel I belonged there, that I was in a house that could be mine. I thought there was a chance we would move to Sheepshead Bay with my mother; this was the section of my life I had been waiting for.

I'd gone from barely having a home of my own in Ivy Hill to having two now, and I snuggled deeper into my sheets, grateful for my new arrangement, and also a little on my guard lest it be taken away.

Outside the bedroom window, car after car passed. I fell asleep listening to them, daring myself to think about the drivers, how none of them knew I was inside, hearing each one of them pass, watching the shadows from their headlights move across my borrowed room.

Family Photos

Mom and Dad in Israel – she's pregnant with me.

My mother and me on the kibbutz.

My mother, father, and me in Jerusalem.

Me, walking a kibbutz path.

My father helping me paint in front of our Kibbutz Lahav home.

Our family our first few months in Seattle.

My sister and me on the steps of the yellow rental house in Seattle, in the final months of my parents living under the same roof.

My sister and me playing in our Seattle backyard after my father moved to New Jersey.

My sister and I dressing up in Ivy Hill, me in Tracy's clothes, and
my sister in my father's clothes.

A visit with my mother in Ivy Hill, soon after she
returned from India.

My sister, mother, and me at our Flushing apartment before a weekend visit when she was still wearing her Bhagwan mala.

Me, my father, and my sister in Flushing when I was eleven.

Serving my father a dinner I cooked.

My mother, sister, and I on a visit day at sleep away camp the
summer before she went to Bhagwan's Oregon ashram.

The three of us at my Bat Mitzvah reception. I'm in 8th grade, my
sister in 5th.

Hand-Me-Downed

It was a bad morning, and nothing I put on felt right. I had laid my blouse and skirt out the night before, but now they were on the floor with the rest of the clothes I'd thrown there.

Skirts and their hangers were scattered on Nava's side of the room, and a scratchy wool sweater lay crumpled in the corner. I'd tossed four missing-button blouses on the bed, and all the pants I owned were heaped in a pile like the castoffs they were—twice cast-off, in fact, hand-me-downs from Sarah and Janine.

I wore blouses with ruffles at the collar, cotton turtlenecks in primary colors, and today, a heavy sweater in the color of Dijon mustard that only one percent of the world's population can pull off without looking sick-to-their-stomach green. I insisted on wearing it only because I hadn't yet stained it.

I chose skirts most of the time: prairie skirts with flowers, corduroy, wool, and my favorite—the one I picked out for today—a navy blue in three tiers with pale pink ribbon separating each panel and small but defined flowers dotted across the good cotton. But the button on the waist, like those on all the skirts from Sarah, wouldn't close around my thicker middle. I could pull the zipper up most of the way but was not able to get the button to meet its buttonhole across the bulge of my stomach.

We had to leave for school in ten minutes and I hadn't even had breakfast yet. I sucked in my breath to close my skirt, then sucked it in more, but I couldn't get the sides together. I shook my hands out, and choking back a sob, gathered the two sides and tried again.

I grabbed a safety pin and lay down on my bed. I collected safety pins whenever I found them around the house and added them to my private supply, especially the big ones, for times like these. I inhaled as much as I could and brought the two sides of the flowered waistline of the skirt together. Finally, trying not to pinch my skin, I fastened the safety pin closed.

I puffed the sweater over the waistline so that people at school wouldn't see my fat squishing over the top of my skirt. As long as the safety pin didn't pop open, I would be all right. Nobody would know I was too big for my clothes.

I was already sweating in my thick mustard turtleneck. (God, that sweater drove me nuts. I wore it again and again, even when the weather warmed up that spring because I knew it was better quality than my other clothing.) But I still had to deal with my hair. I held up a front section and clipped it into a barrette but there was a bump. I unclipped the barrette, swept my hair up again, and clipped the barrette. I saw a new bump. I unclipped the barrette and tried again. My hair was always the part of getting ready for the day that could do me in. I wished my mother was there to help me.

I had to drop my arms to give them a break; they were getting tired from holding my hair up into the shape I wanted. Standing in front of my dresser mirror, my stomach spilling over the safety-pinned waist of my skirt, the crotch of my scratchy tights sinking lower and lower because I had outgrown them, I wanted to scream and fling myself on my bed, rip everything off. Why didn't I look the way I wanted to? Why didn't I feel the way I wanted to feel? What did I have to do to be okay?

I couldn't figure out how to soothe myself, and my father and Nava certainly didn't know how to either. They each walked up to the bedroom doorway, saw my red face and my whirligig eyes and backed out immediately.

I took out both my barrettes and pulled the brush through my tangles, chewing on my lip to try to regain some control. No matter how many times I tried, I couldn't get my barrette in my hair the way I wanted. My neck was itchy and prickling, the heat building, forming into a sheen of sweat on my forehead and beginning to bead over my top lip.

Nava came by again to drop off the stuffed bunny she was holding and get her glasses from her dresser, and I wanted to kick her because she'd crossed my path—because she seemed fine and I wasn't.

I finished getting ready—I did what I was supposed to do, like I always did—but I felt like I was collapsing inside.

I rushed through my breakfast, dribbling milk from my cereal onto my sweater and patting it into the fabric, satisfied it had disappeared. I didn't realize that when Nava and I got outside that the splotches showed in the daylight. We walked to school with me sulking ahead of her, my bangs flapping in my eyes. I was deeply unsettled and looking for a target. Anything she said I ignored; anything she asked me I answered in a grunt.

If I couldn't fit into a tenth-graders clothing—even if Sarah was slender and small-framed—then I was the problem, not the skirts. I was embarrassed and I don't think I ever told my father I had trouble with my clothes. He assumed I was fine because I always had my morning tasks done and was ready for school when I needed to be.

My responsibilities were getting myself ready, helping Nava with her hair and outfits, and bringing coffee to my father.

I don't know how my bringing him coffee began, if I thought that was what I was supposed to do or if he had encouraged it. I'm sure a part of me felt I had to make sure our new living arrangements worked and that he was happy.

Every morning at 7:30 I boiled the water and poured it over two teaspoons of instant Folgers and two teaspoons of sugar, then added a splash of half-and-half. I'd walk with halting steps so the coffee wouldn't slop over the mug's rim, past the bedroom I shared with

Nava, who was still asleep, cross the dining room, and knock on his door. When he called out for me to come in, I'd switch the mug to my right hand, trying not to burn my palms, and turn the knob with my left. I'd try to glide across the floor without picking up my heels, concentrating on holding the mug steady until I made it over to where he lay in his bed, the blanket covering him to his waist.

"Good morning, Dad!" I'd say, handing him his mug.

"Thank you, kid," he'd say, sitting up in bed and putting his glasses on. I would chatter about what was still left to do to get ready for school, and then I'd leave. But before I was all the way out of the room, I'd say, "Are you sure you're awake?" and only after he answered, "Yeah, kid," or "I'm awake," would I leave.

Maybe I felt I was standing in for Tracy, taking over in making sure my father was satisfied. Or maybe I felt caring for everybody was my responsibility. Whatever the reason, I kept up my morning coffee duties for years.

~

By the time I was eleven I was doing a lot of the laundry, taking over some of the grocery shopping, and making dinner for our family. Spaghetti and burned steak, canned peas and hamburgers, things like that.

Despite the grown-up tasks, in so many ways living with my father was good. He genuinely enjoyed talking with me and Nava, hearing our perspectives and learning about our school days and our friends. "I get a kick out of you two," he'd say. He paid attention to our stories, laughed at our jokes, and told us how proud he was to be our father. When we wanted permission to do something, like have a sleepover or go somewhere new with a friend, he encouraged us to state our case confidently and clearly. "I don't want to raise whiny kids," he said.

After working all day in the city, he still helped us with our homework and spent time tucking us in at night. He'd tell Nava bedtime stories he made up, and I listened in. After he had stroked each of our heads and given us a kiss on the cheek goodnight, he'd leave the bedroom door slightly ajar so we could see the hall light. I'd sing lullabies to Nava when she had trouble falling asleep and I felt safe those nights; at peace inside and satisfied with our life.

Even so, living in Flushing wasn't ideal. Stray cats screeched as they fought in the alley outside our windows at night and this apartment had roaches, too. Even when the exterminator sprayed for them—a service we signed up for regularly, because if others in the building sprayed but we didn't, who knew how many roaches would show up at our place—it didn't solve the problem for long.

For a few days after the exterminator had been in the apartment, leaving behind a chemical-y, maple-syrupy smell, the roaches would hide away. But then, sure enough, a few nights later when I turned on the kitchen or bathroom light, I'd see the brown-shelled bodies in small and big sizes go scurrying into the cracks and seams of the tile. I learned to turn my head when I flipped the light switch or shut my eyes so I could pretend they weren't there.

One day in school, I noticed itching on the sole of my right foot. I sat at my desk stamping and stamping my foot to stop the tickling sensation. About halfway to lunchtime, I decided to take my shoe off and really scratch the arch of my foot once and for all. I bent down and unbuckled my Mary Jane, and before I had taken it all the way off, a medium-sized roach crawled out of it. I jumped in my seat and shrieked before I realized I should keep quiet. I knew I couldn't let on that roaches were hitching rides with me to school. My heart thumping, I looked around and tried to act like nothing had happened.

Roaches were an insult, a reminder of how my life had changed. I was from dewy green Seattle and the baking Negev Desert. My mother had made decisions; my father had made decisions. All of which had led me here.

Guilt Bubble

That winter my father took Nava and me to Elizabeth, New Jersey, to visit Tracy and her girls. I was nine-and-a-half years old now and it had been many months since I'd seen them, but my father had kept in touch with Tracy. Perhaps they were friends or maybe they were still occasionally dating. I don't know much about their relationship.

Halfheartedly, the girls showed us around their new apartment. I wondered if now that some time had passed Sarah might like me better, but it didn't appear that things had changed.

Tracy had decided to order pizza for dinner, but there was no delivery nearby so she and Janine said they'd pick it up. I volunteered to join them. I was in fourth grade now—much more mature, I thought, than when they'd first known me—and bringing back dinner seemed like an older-kid thing to do.

It was dark out and snowflakes were lightly falling. The night seemed otherworldly, the streets and sidewalks almost beautiful, the layer of snow softening the edges of this poor, unremarkable neighborhood, as if the town were under a spell.

The sidewalks were slick. We chose our steps carefully at first, placing one foot on the ground and making sure it was firmly planted before lifting the other one to avoid slipping. Intermittent streetlamps cast their cold, white light onto the road and empty sidewalks. No cars passed. It was a late-night adventure, I thought, and I was being helpful, maybe proving my worth to Janine and Tracy.

We turned onto a street where the road was empty except for a few parked cars and a bus stop where no one was waiting. Across the street was a cemetery behind high wrought iron bars; it looked enchanted but eerie, emitting a gray glowing light.

We walked in step, three across; Tracy was in the middle, Janine and I on either side of her, huddling together against the cold. Just then a figure darted out from the cemetery gate. A man. He swiped at Tracy's purse and she screamed. He pulled at it and Tracy held it tighter. She sunk low and dug in her heels but the snow made it hard to steady herself. He tugged at the purse, she held onto the strap, and this is how he pulled her, her shoes skidding in the new sidewalk slush, dragging her almost like she was jet skiing behind him.

Janine rushed over to her mother. "Stop!" she shrieked at the man. "Stop it!" and she yanked back on the purse strap with Tracy.

I didn't understand what I was seeing. It almost looked like they were playing a game. The whole thing seemed to occur in slow motion, five seconds behind the actual action, my brain still trying to register what was happening.

I backed into a phone booth with a missing a door. I knew I should help in some way but was scared of getting hurt. I was grateful for the safety of the spotlight from the streetlamp above me and also scared I would be conspicuous in its glare.

I huddled inside, worried the mugger was going to discover me hiding and come after me next. As the scene went silent, I drifted out of my body. I could only piece together the scene in fragments, like in comic book panels. His punch to Janine's nose. His kick to Tracy's head. My distance from them. His maroon knit hat. The snow falling. The ghostly light from the blue-white dusted grass in the cemetery. The smallness of being alone.

I didn't know where I would go if something worse happened to Tracy and Janine, if he hurt them so badly they couldn't help me.

Which street had we walked up from? No cars had passed but if they did how would I know I could trust the drivers? Could I ask for help? I didn't know Tracy's address. I didn't know their phone number. I didn't have coins in my pocket for the pay phone.

Sound returned. I heard Janine cry out. Tracy had fallen onto the snow. The man disappeared across the street. He had Tracy's purse.

I knew that you should always just give up your purse if you're mugged. What was Tracy, this tiny lady, doing clutching at her leather strap, trying to pull it to her chest when there was herself and two girls to take care of? In the moment, I couldn't decide if her actions were brave or irresponsible.

Tracy stood up and Janine clung to her. I took a few steps out of my phone booth, and when they began walking, I joined them. We didn't talk on the way home. Janine sobbed and Tracy put her arm around her. I walked next to them in a guilt bubble, knowing I was deadweight, relieved I hadn't been hurt but aware that was because I was a coward. Being unharmed was like a mark against me; in a way I knew I would feel better if I, too, had suffered. I knew I wasn't responsible but I hadn't even tried to help.

I scanned ahead as we walked back to the apartment, peering at bushes we passed, craning my neck in the dark to see around the mailbox, the trees, as if my alertness could make up for my having done nothing before.

When we got back Janine told the others what had happened but their eyes looked uncomprehending, so I took over.

"The man came from somewhere by the cemetery," I burst in.

Tracy and Janine didn't say anything, so I babbled on, filling the shock in the apartment with the sound of my voice, with words; sharing details that Tracy and Janine couldn't remember or weren't able to talk about. What had begun as a little adventure on a night of our reunion had turned into a terrible memory, a terrible night.

~

For my birthday, just after fourth grade started, my father surprised me with a kitten. It's what I had wanted since the first time I saw one

114

on the kibbutz when I was two. He brought her home in a cardboard carrier from the animal shelter. She must have been a Russian Blue mix, because she was a deep gray with amber eyes. I named her Misty and she was little, only eight weeks old.

I held her close to my neck but she didn't stay still long and wriggled out of my arms. I played with her, though she didn't bat at the ribbon I pulled along the floor or chase the balls of aluminum foil I made, after consulting a book on kittens I had checked out from the library. I kept her litter box immaculate and fed her when I was supposed to, but she wasn't well. She was already taking amoxicillin for a cold but was losing weight and starting to have stomach troubles all over the house. The vet we brought her to recommended we feed her a combination of white rice, grape jelly, jarred baby food, and little pieces of steak until her stomach was better. Though this seemed a little complicated when the vet first suggested it, I would do whatever he said to prove I was good at taking care of small creatures. I had written down the instructions and amounts, and at every feeding time I pulled out the ingredients I needed and mixed up her special food.

Misty started to do better after two weeks, but she was twitchy. She was hunched and watchful and her tail was in motion even when she sat still. She didn't play the way I had imagined a kitten would, but I picked her up and attempted to cuddle her and put her in our bedroom at night. When she got confident enough to make it to the top bunk where I slept, she'd leap up to where I lay and jump all over me, which I took as a sign of affection. She attacked my feet, stalked and chomped on my toes, bit my hands, and scratched my arms. I didn't think it was okay that I was getting hurt, but it wasn't unbearable; at least she was spending time with me.

Every night, after my father tucked us in and turned out the lights, I anticipated her arrival with nervous hope. I half-hid under the covers, butterflies in my stomach, happy she would visit me, bracing myself for the pain, optimistic that eventually she'd settle down and cuddle with me.

Months went by and the scratches on my arms grew in number.

The thin lines were different colors, from fresh pink with scabs to faded brown, depending on the time of injury. When adults or classmates asked me about them, I'd tilt my head to the side and roll my eyes. "It's from my kitten," I'd tell them in mock exasperation, proud that I could say I had a kitten in the first place. Almost as if I was lucky to be the recipient of such attention, that it was simply the price I had to pay for living with a baby animal. If I thought it was getting out of hand or not that much fun anymore, I didn't admit it. I didn't want to tell my father. I didn't want him to get mad at Misty or make me give her away. When he asked me about the scratches I responded as glibly as I could that I was fine, that's how kittens played.

Perhaps my father had forgotten to make Misty's spay appointment or didn't think it was a problem to skip it, but after we'd had her for about seven months she went into heat. I watched in horror as she yowled and cried around the house with increasing frenzy. She'd slink around, transformed into this new sexual creature, rubbing her face on my father's socks, laying on the T-shirts he'd left on his bedroom rug, shoving her nose into its armpit. This was a big deal. To me the sexuality of it was grotesque. She seemed piqued by my father's scent and I was disturbed by this. I wanted my kitten to be innocent, I wanted my home to be cozy and safe. I reminded my father we had to take her in to the vet for the procedure.

Then one early evening Nava, who was seven years old by now, was in the living room with me. She crossed the room toward the window and when she passed, Misty sprung at her from the corner where she had been crouched. She sunk her front claws into Nava's back and, hanging there, bit into her. Nava didn't understand what was happening and screamed. She swiped at her back and Misty, still dangling from Nava, bit her again. Nava, stunned by the ambush, kept screaming, but couldn't move and Misty lost her grip and dropped to the floor.

I went to Nava and shooed Misty away from her just as my father ran in to see what had happened. "That's it," my father said, without hesitation, and he picked Misty up and locked her in his bedroom. I knew it was bad. Later that night my father told me we couldn't keep the cat and he would take her to the vet the next day.

The following morning, I said goodbye to Misty, and Nava and I went to school. I was mad at my father and annoyed at Nava, but not deeply. I knew she felt guilty for what had happened and I didn't make it worse for her. A part of me knew that Misty wasn't a good cat for me. A part of me felt relief to be done trying to make it work.

Even when I tried to write about losing Misty for a school assignment and how she was going to be put down, I couldn't tell if I was sad enough. If Misty was mine to care for, how could my life so easily go on without her? It bothered me that I could forget about her—I wasn't sure what that said about who I was and whether my mother had felt the same about me.

Misty was gone and I didn't have to worry about her scratching me anymore. Our life went back to the way it had been and the marks on my arms eventually faded. It was like she had never been there.

Perfect for Kids

Soon after Grandma Lina died my mother became a devotee and recruiter for Erhard Seminars Training, or as they branded it, *Est*. Erhard Seminars Training, like Bhagwan's teachings, was an offshoot of the Human Potential Movement and was founded by Werner Erhard, the name assumed by Philadelphia-born used-car salesman Jack Rosenberg. "Werner," as his followers referred to him, promised personal transformation, claiming that in just sixty hours and $250 (in the 1980s) spent over the course of two weekends of seminars, he could awaken one's authentic spiritual identity. His catchphrases had a paradoxical-like quality—"What is, is, and what isn't, isn't," and ultimately, about 700,000 people attended his seminars, which eventually morphed into the Forum and then later Landmark Worldwide.

But in 1983 Est was still going strong. On weekends my mother had Nava and me with her, she would bring us with her to Est's Manhattan headquarters, a building in the mid-30s on the east side near the Midtown Tunnel, to work her shift helping to recruit people and attend trainings herself so she could advance.

Nava and I spent those hours on the newly laid, gray industrial carpet, looking for ways to pass the time. While my mother went to a different part of the building to attend seminars and pep talks, and

118

adults with headsets manned phones on the desks above us, we played "office" with a dead phone, pretended to sell each other things, stapled together whatever loose sheets of copy paper we could find, and used a working phone to crank call a few New Yorkers. When we tired of that we tried to make up new games, but after several hours there was nothing left to do.

This was one of the only times I allowed myself an eye-roll about my mother. Where was she? Why'd we have to come to this place with her, and when would she come back? I didn't get as far as anger but it was as close to frustrated as I had ever admitted feeling about her. When she finally came to get us, I was slow to warm. I wouldn't directly say how I was feeling, but I wanted her to know that it wasn't right for her to spend so much time on herself during the weekends she was supposed to focus on us.

I broke up the time by making trips to the bathroom and pretending I had my period, which I was years away from getting. I unwrapped maxi pads and examined tampons the Est people had stocked the bathroom with, trying to figure out how they worked, just in case. I froze in my stall whenever the door opened and a woman came in, making sure not to rustle the maxi pad wrapper until I heard them leave. Then, as soon as the door shut behind them, I'd pick up where I left off, pretending I'd hit puberty and was now transformed into the grown up and improved version of myself I so longed to be.

Once, on my way back to Nava, I got to look into a room I'd never seen, where they must have held special meetings. A blond woman with short hair flashed me a smile from inside as she approached the door to close it. Before she did, I saw the room was painted lavender. A rainbow in fat brushstrokes decorated the back wall; below it was a plush red sofa. A single lamp glowed warm orange on a side table, a purple beanbag chair next to it. It was beautiful. Had my mother ever been in that room? I wanted to be there, not the sterile white room where Nava and I had to wait. I didn't know why we couldn't at least spend a little time in the cozy rainbow room.

My mother went to a lot of meetings and adopted the jargon of the movement. She told Nava and me that we had to "Acknowledge" our behavior and "Own It" and then, and only then, would we "Get It." *It* being the magical level of emotional intelligence or serenity Est devotees aspired to—a state of mind, a consciousness which would free them from their basic lives, their stuckness. And for my mother, it seemed, to help her escape from the parts of herself she deemed unworthy or weak. When she was doing Est I think she would have described herself as empowered and independent. I saw that in her too—especially because she carried herself with confidence and presented herself to the outside word that way.

A part of me can relate to that need to find something to believe in. For a long time as a young adult, I thought if I could just find my true path, whether that meant discovering the right career or the right people to learn from, the right spirituality, even the exact right quote, I would unlock my true self. I got into astrology and crystals for a while, and in college at State University of New York (SUNY) Binghamton when I was nineteen, I tried Wicca. I even found a student coven to join. My evenings there didn't feel completely fulfilling, but I believed Wicca would bring about my *aha* moment, the breakthrough that would change my life and set me on my ultimate course.

After meeting with that student coven every other week for a few months, I decided to join a community-wide coven celebration for Candlemas that the Unitarian church was hosting on the first of February. I wanted to live like a true Wiccan and prove my commitment to my newly-chosen path.

I walked to the church by myself in the icy night, confident the Goddess would keep me safe, and entered the great hall of the church. Beams of wood cut high across the ceiling and met at a center point far above my head; several hundred pagans milled around the room dressed in everything from stone-washed jeans to richly-hued crushed velvet robes. Some wore chunky silver pentacles, others delicate crystal pendants, and little gusts of patchouli and sandalwood hit me as they passed. I didn't see anyone from my study coven and was feeling self-conscious when the lights dimmed. Men began pounding animal skin drums and I joined the circle forming on the outer edges of the great room.

Wiccans were dancing on the perimeter and I was trying to get into it even though I've never really liked dancing much and definitely not in public. I clapped to the beat unsure what we were all facing the inside of the circle for when a shirtless young man in black tights and a hint of a mullet entered the circle. He strutted in smiling mischievously and ladies in the crowd whooped and whistled; a few women threw flowers at him. The drummers drummed louder and now the circle really began thrumming. Then, in what seemed to be one fluid movement, he popped a giant rack of antlers someone had passed him onto his head and leapt into the middle of the circle.

He spun, he pranced, he undulated, moving like the stag he now was, kicking his foot-hooves at the ground, and the crowd went wild.

I clapped along and shouted a weak, "Woo hoo," and I bobbed my head to the beat. I tried to let go, to get excited about this half-naked guy-as-deer but I couldn't seem to lose myself. I thought I was ready to embrace my new practice, I thought I was open-minded, but seeing all these people behave in concert, focused on the same one thing, made me uncomfortable. Too performative for my tastes, too forced; the gathering was not for me. I simply didn't have it in me to give myself over in this way. I backed out of the drum circle just as the Stag God lowered his head, heaved his antlers from side to side, and made his way to a woman in the circle. I slipped outside, back into the freezing February air, and walked home. That was the end of my Wicca exploration.

Maybe I inherited an impulse for spiritual pursuits from my mother, but one of the crucial differences between us is that my mother had never really been made to feel accepted in her family, so she sought that out in groups. I grew up with a sense of belonging, thanks to my father who made it clear I was protected and cared for. This may be what stopped me from diving in all the way. I've always had a shut off valve.

~

About the same time my mother did Est she started dating Sean, who was from Ireland and played piano at local pubs and restaurants. He liked her a lot. Up until this point I hadn't met any of the men in her life, but she was renting an apartment in the city for the summer with him to see how they liked living together, and we saw him some of the weekends we were with her.

The apartment had one bedroom, and when we visited, Nava and I stayed on the pull-out sofa. One Saturday morning, after calling for my mother and getting no response, I walked into the bedroom to look for her but found only Sean there. He appeared to have just swung his legs over his side of the bed when I walked in and was hurrying to cover himself up, pulling the top sheet over his lap. It was hard to get my eyes to adjust at first, with the bright morning sun spilling in from the high windows of the pre-war apartment, but when they did I fixated on the carpet of his chest. Never had I encountered a man so ruddy-skinned and furry.

He was the first man other than my father I had ever seen shirtless in bed but I was more curious than intimidated. I was nine-and-a-half and wondered if to him I was just a little girl making a mistake, or a bigger girl capable of embarrassing him. He leaned over and rested his elbows on his thighs, then ran a hand through his reddish blond hair, combing it back from his eyes. He didn't exactly smile at me but his lips moved to the side a little. He didn't appear angry—more surprised. Maybe he was a little unsure of how he should react. He seemed to be choosing not to make a big deal that I had found him this way, in the bed he shared with my mother, naked. And I played along. Most of my childhood I did my best to look in control, to act like nothing much surprised me. I remember both being aware of making a choice to take this awkward encounter in stride and that a part of me was challenging him to see how he would handle the situation. Nava and I only saw him twice more before they broke up.

My mother officially moved out of Sheepshead Bay and into Manhattan after she and her brother and sister sold Grandma Lina's house. She still had her job working for the communications company in the city. She cut her hair short and sleek and put on full makeup every day; she bought chic clothes, more expensive perfume. She didn't wear her Bhagwan necklace anymore, which pleased me. For me it was the beginning of my mother claiming her position in my life. I had guarded that space for her, defended our original nest.

I was happy to count on our weekends together, going out to eat and then later lounging around in pajamas with her and Nava, just the three of us. Now that we were seeing her regularly, I began to relax more during my time with her. And she, perhaps settling into her new, grown up New York life, always planned things for us to do on the weekends. When we weren't at Est she took us to museums and art exhibits, to the East Village for Indian food, to Central Park to watch break-dancers. We walked through street fairs teeming with New Yorkers—the beautiful, the average, and the run-down—the sound of music from boom boxes thumping the smell of smoke and kebabs around us, giant garbage bags heaped on the corners, and occasional fire engines screaming by. Though I was at times overwhelmed by the sights and sounds and the sheer mass of people, these are some of my clearest and best memories of time with my mother.

We stayed up late eating snacks and watching Saturday Night Live, and sometimes I could get her to take out her Tarot cards, which she'd learned how to read in India. I wanted to know what my future held and who I would marry, if I would finally meet Christopher Reeve, whom I fell in love with when she took us to see *Superman II*, and if I was doomed to have chubby cheeks my whole life. Tarot readings were the only times I was curious about my mother's time away from us in India. But we didn't talk about Bhagwan or the ashram—those days were in the past, and I wanted them to stay there.

My mother's apartment on East 29th Street in the Murray Hill area was small but pretty and clean, so different from where we lived with my father. It was also the first place of her own I had seen, designed with only her in mind. She lay out a silver-threaded scarf from her time on the ashram on her dresser and covered it with quartz crystals and pieces of amethyst. She placed sunset-colored candles in the shapes of pyramids there too. From the futon on the floor where Nava and I slept on weekends, I would stare at the range of colors, working from the base of the pyramids up: sienna to orange to blush to yellow on one, purple to indigo to violet to pink on the other, trying to find the exact place on the candle the color changed. These objects reflected who she was when I wasn't with her—a woman on her own in the city and seemingly happy; a time and place I had no part of. Yet everything looked so perfect, so exactly the way I might want my life to look as a woman.

She had creamy, scented lotions in her bathroom cabinet and she decorated her shelves with figurines and pottery. She placed small baskets in different sizes in her bathroom and on her dresser to hold earrings, necklaces, cotton balls. The tight weave on the baskets reminded me of a Triscuit cracker, and they had a sweet hay smell. These things were chosen by and belonged to this woman who was my mother, and I wanted to touch and hold them. I wanted to absorb them, soak them in, find a map of her and of myself within them.

Was I going to be similar to her? Did I want to be? Because she was with me again, I had the luxury of assessing her. I gave myself permission to evaluate the freckles and moles on her arms and neck, and I determined she had too many. I could decide if I liked her clothes—if, when I grew up, I would wear outfits like hers or not. If I would go out dancing at night, if I would have hairy men in my bed. I had no idea then that having her near me was not something I should begin to take for granted.

My mother had traveled thousands upon thousands of miles in search of herself. She'd followed a guru, shacked up with an Indian lover, and read Tarot cards to pay her rent. Now, back in New York, she had an apartment and a job but was still searching for some deeper calling, for a sense of purpose. She ran a marathon; she walked on hot coals, she jumped out of an airplane and before she found Est she got involved with a multi-level marketing company called Neo-Life that sold nutritional supplements.

But following Est was like following Bhagwan in that the change the movement promised hinged on followers giving themselves over to a leader who told them what to do. In order to attain liberation from their old patterns and transcend the trappings of their material lives, they had to meticulously create and adhere to new patterns invented by a leader they weren't supposed to question. Self-empowerment was the lure but many of those who bought in ended up losing themselves and hurting the people who cared about them the most.

One Friday night during my mother's Est period she picked Nava and me up in Flushing like usual. After we'd eaten McDonald's, she took us with her to a party some people from the Est community were throwing in the city. It was almost nine o'clock when we got off the subway near Central Park.

Up the cement steps, black-spotted from decades of discarded gum, the hot mineral and urine smell rising from the subway platform gave way to sweltry summer air. My mother paused to get her bearings. Across the street giant linden trees loomed, towering over the low stone walls that separated the park from the city, their leaves fluttering in the breeze, their honeyed blossoms scenting the air—so sweet, so cloying, it reminded me of the urine in the subway below.

We'd made it only half a block when a man started yelling at us from about thirty feet behind. My mother brought Nava in closer under her arm and walked faster. I kept up on her other side.

"How far away is it, Mom?" I asked. I didn't know which apartment building we were going to, but I knew we had to get there soon or we would be in trouble. The mugging in New Jersey when I was with Tracy and Janine had also happened on a dark, empty street.

She looked at the scrap of paper in her hand. "We're almost there."

We walked faster.

"But which one is it?"

She didn't answer.

I looked over my shoulder, stumbling as we picked up the pace to nearly a trot. The man grew closer every few seconds, closing the distance, hollering and pointing his finger at us. He swung his head side to side in an almost exasperated way, like he couldn't believe he had to keep repeating whatever it was he was shouting about in order for us to understand. There seemed to be nobody else on the block, and in my view, we were the perfect target for him, for anyone who would want to hurt us. I wasn't sure this man was as dangerous as the mugger that night with Tracy and Janine, but because I had been in this kind of position before I had no delusions that my mother would be able to protect us or herself—whereas if we were with our father, I figured he could at least try to physically overpower our pursuer.

Finally, we made it to the awning of a sandy-colored, eighteen-story building.

My mother reached for the lobby door but it was locked. "Shit!" she said.

"Come on!" the man behind us shouted, "Come on!" I huddled near my mother and snuck a look back at him. He was getting closer.

My mother pressed and pressed the button to get buzzed inside, then double-checked the address. I hid behind her as best I could so the man wouldn't see me. If these people didn't let us in, I didn't know what was going to happen.

Finally, the buzzer sounded and the door clicked open. I didn't look back until the door clicked closed again, my body tensing all over again as the man continued shouting and waving his arms at us from outside the glass. The three of us got into the elevator and I didn't look up from where I huddled next to my mother and Nava. We rode the elevator in silence, the only sounds that of the cables creaking on the way to the eighth floor.

That silence we all consciously or unconsciously committed to kept me worried as we stepped out of the elevator, walked down the hallway and knocked on the apartment door. If my mother had told us everything would be okay or made a joke, if *any* of us had cracked a joke, it would have broken the spell. But we didn't talk about the man or the danger he represented. My mother didn't offer insight into how she felt; not a word.

In my family, we didn't say, "You seem upset," or, "It's scary to have a man follow you," or, "It's sad to see your mom only every two weeks." But not recognizing an experience or acknowledging a feeling doesn't shrink them down to nothing. Feelings that go unnamed grow bigger. They can swallow you. And tonight, I didn't feel safe or secure. The world outside had breached my little bubble and I didn't have my mother to hold onto. She didn't seem available to me or I didn't think I could lean on her.

After we walked inside the apartment where the party was, we dropped our overnight bags and my mother's purse in a bedroom where her short, theatrical Est friend, Greg, whose lips shined with fresh gloss, shrieked a high-pitched hello and pulled her away to fill her in on some gossip Nava and I weren't privy too. They whispered together as they made their way to the living room, and Nava and I followed them. Though the lights were low I took note of our surroundings, as I always did: the tall ceilings; the soft-edged, cream-colored baseboard moldings; the plants; the smell of wicker; and the snacks, none of which interested me. All that these people seemed to eat was hummus and vegetables. I heard Greg whisper several women's names and my mother leaned in to hear the story. I was tired. Without speaking, Nava and I knew that we were stuck. Tonight, as usual, we were the only children and we didn't know anyone at the party. I tried to stay close to my mother, and Nava stayed close to me, but I didn't know where to put myself.

I stood near the snack table, Nava at my arm, my eyes on my mother, who was now on the dance floor—a living room that had been cleared of furniture. Adults walked by with drinks in their hands, occasionally smiling at us as they passed. A woman with dirty blonde hair in clips stopped.

"You having fun?" she asked.

I gave her half a smile.

"Why aren't you dancing?"

I shrugged my shoulders.

"Really, you should dance."

I wanted to scream at her—I wanted to scream at everyone in the room. I hated it when people told me to dance. I didn't even like dancing and certainly didn't want to dance with strangers. I wanted to go back to my mother's studio apartment and get into pajamas and start our weekend together. I wanted to snuggle down for the night in her soft sheets with her nearby. I wanted to be able to believe her when she said, "We'll leave soon." I wanted to be able to trust her.

The people at the party fawned over my mother's outfit; they complimented her on how nice she looked, and I imagine she liked the attention. I admired her, too, the way she seemed confident and exotic. I liked that she knew Tarot and followed her intuition, how in so many ways she seemed wise, but I was not at ease around her. While her limitlessness was a touchstone for her, it troubled me.

When she was on the dance floor, I kept track of her to make sure she was okay, to make sure Nava and I were safe. It was like trying to orbit a planet whose gravitational pull kept changing. We couldn't get too close, since our mother was dancing with her friends, but I didn't want to venture too far away. It felt like it was up to me to make sure she remembered us. That we were with her; that she was supposed to take care of us.

Something was missing: the part of me that had earned her unconditional love and her approval. I had no evidence to the contrary; it was clear I was not enough to capture her attention. And yet, I knew I was also too much: too loud, too sloppy, too anxious, too cold, too insistent. I didn't have that magic ingredient most kids had that captivates and forms the glue of their relationship with their mother. Kids may not realize they have that power over their parents, but they can feel it when it's absent. They scramble, they perform, or maybe they step away and stop trying. But not me. I worked hard to draw my mother in for years and years. I was afraid of her absence, what her being gone could do to Nava and me.

Naked Ladies

The only women Nava and I saw at my father's apartment when we first lived there were in photographs: tiny ones on matchbooks my father got with his cigarette cartons. Each shrunken image I studied was of a different woman, each sharing common qualities: tanned and pretty with long, thick hair in shades of blonde, red, brown, and black—and they were all naked. Their nipples were double bull's-eyes on the paler skin of their breasts, which were outlined, as were their crotches, in the shapes of past bikinis.

My father got those matches from a particular smoke shop on Kissena Boulevard where he bought his Winstons. On one occasion he had Nava and me in tow and the heavyset Pakistani man hesitated before he handed a matchbook over the counter. His eyes shifted from my father to me and then Nava, his fat thumb covering the photo. I wanted to tell him he didn't need to worry about me. I'd seen the naked ladies before.

At the apartment, in the hours my father was at work and we were alone, Nava and I hunted out those matches wherever we thought we might find them. It was like a game. When we saw a new pack, we would grab a blue ballpoint pen—ink worked better than markers—and press hard into the flimsy cardboard, scribbling over the naked ladies' private parts, to give them back at least a little dignity. I think I wanted my father to know Nava and I were watching and he couldn't hide what he did, especially from me. If he picked up an edited matchbook Nava and I would shoot each other a look and one of us would ask if he noticed anything different about the photo and he would kind of smirk. Or, if he was looking for a book of matches around the apartment and I dangled one in front of him, so he could see what Nava and I had done, he'd shake his head and hold out his hand and say something like, "Give me that, you rotten kid."

~

About a year after we moved to Flushing my father began to date. I could tell the nights he was having a woman over because he acted differently. Once evening came my antennae were up, looking for signals, picking up subtle changes in his behavior, like his rushing through our bedtime routine or acting distracted.

Once when my father tucked us in and said goodnight, I was brave enough to ask, "Who's coming over?" I felt the tension change between us.

"A friend," he said.

I could tell by the way he tilted his head slightly and the strain in his voice, that I shouldn't push for more. "A friend," I decided, meant more than a friend. Because if the visitor was a friend, why was her visit a secret, and why did she arrive late at night? That was not a friend. In the absence of further detail, my mind couldn't rest. Who was she? The same person, over and over? Had he called in a prostitute? I'd heard of those. Was it Tracy and, if so, why couldn't he say he was still seeing her?

On these nights, instead of leaving our bedroom door propped open, my father would close it all the way. From the moment he shut it I would sit up in bed and listen for our heavy front door, straining to hear a murmur, a laugh, the click of high heels. I'd ask Nava to stay up so she could go out and ask my father for a glass of water after the visitor arrived and spy for me, but soon she drifted to sleep and I was left alone. It didn't seem to bother her the way it bothered me.

I would go mad with the not knowing, with the world hidden from me. For me, information was safety, and my father's secrecy didn't make sense. He put me in charge of taking care of my sister, and I cooked all our dinners and did a lot of the shopping when we went to the grocery store. He asked my advice on his coworkers, he shared so much with me about his adult life—so why not this? In many ways he treated me as if I were a friend or partner, rather than a daughter, an adult instead of an elementary school kid, but each time he shut my bedroom door against his rendezvous in the living room, he turned me into a child again, put me in my place. I hated being left out. I was insulted that he thought I was stupid enough to not notice that only ten minutes after he said goodnight to us, a stranger came to our door.

Did she leave at midnight? I don't think the women hid in his bedroom the next morning, because I was still serving my father coffee in bed and he was always alone when I went in. I would place his mug on his night table and wish him a good morning, and he would thank me. I would scan the room on my way out for a woman's shoe, a purse, anything out of place. The other side of the bed was, as usual, empty.

The first of three women he allowed my sister and me to meet was Barbara. She was tall, with dark curly hair like my mother, but pretty in a plainer way. She smiled a lot and laughed loudly. There was garishness about her. We saw her only a handful of times, but in the short period my father dated Barbara she managed to infiltrate our newly-established life in Flushing pretty successfully. The first afternoon she settled neatly into the corner of our couch with her knees tucked under her in a cozy pose, her bushy hair sprouting from her head. She looked like she thought she belonged there. As if she had won a prize.

I felt myself harden inside, resisting her apparent ease in inhabiting our space. I was like a sentinel guarding my family of three, as if I had a say in who would stay and who could go. In my mind, I had to be the protector—this was my family, my life.

One Saturday afternoon my father called me into his office and handed me the phone. "Barbara wants to speak with you," he said. I felt proud that she had specifically asked for me, but caught off guard that he was allowing her to communicate with me on her own.

"I'm coming over with a surprise," she told me. "But I don't want your dad to know. Can you buzz me in when I ring up?" I was thrown by this conspiratorial turn of events, but I agreed. Was Barbara recruiting me as an ally?

I doubted her surprise would please me or Nava—nothing like donuts or a new kitten to replace Misty—as she said her gift was meant for my father. But I was intrigued. And part of me was impressed that she had wised up enough to know that she'd have to get on my good side if she wanted to be part of our family. I decided, as if I were bestowing an honor, that I was prepared to accept her offer.

The buzzer rang over the intercom and she told me to be ready to open the apartment door for her. When I did, she stood there wearing a formal, off-the-shoulder, ruffled burgundy gown made of taffeta. She put her finger to her lips and giggled. I looked into the carpeted hallway behind her. She had no bakery boxes with her, no kittens, just as I'd predicted. Her getup was the surprise.

The dress made noise when she gathered it up in her hands and swooshed into the apartment, the stiff fabric rubbing crisply against our chalk-white foyer walls. She flounced in, so proud of herself with her fluffy short hair that I felt like telling her that her giant eyeglasses ruined the look. She flitted over to my father's bedroom and knocked; I trailed behind and watched from the dining room. When he opened the door and saw Barbara there, her figure almost completely filling his doorway, she burst into giggles again. He looked surprised. It was like she had told him a joke he didn't get.

Still, he complimented her. She blushed and I scanned his face to see if he was just trying to make her feel good—certainly he couldn't be falling for this woman. But then she disappeared inside. I drifted over to the living room. After another few minutes his bedroom door closed, and I joined Nava in our room, irritated with Barbara for involving me in her game, whatever it was, angry again that the two of them had shut me out—and that she had ignored me as soon as she had gained entry to the apartment.

I hated the way she played the coquette around my father, her lilting laugh and her head tossed as if she were a horse, her curly hair flying. Most of the time I observed her with politeness, but I felt ruthless toward her; a place inside of me that wouldn't budge, which I now recognize as fear. I could not take a personality in the house larger than myself; I could not risk being forgotten. When he broke up with her, I felt vindicated and calm again.

Maybe I would have competed for my father's attention with my mother, too, if she'd been around. Or maybe these strange women angered me because they were not my other parent. The animosity I had toward not just Barbara but anyone who garnered my father's interest was partly because they were interrupting our single-dad home, partly because they were maternal imposters. Maybe, like a homing pigeon or salmon returning to spawn, I was acting on simple instinct: I would resist any woman who wasn't my mom.

Hazy at the Edges

We were in San Diego visiting my father's mother, Grandma Doris, the summer I was almost eleven. She and her second husband Saul had moved to San Diego from New York for the warm weather after she had undergone some heart surgeries. She was still not in good shape and didn't venture far from her condo, except when she took trips to Vegas to play the slots. She wore a housedress over her soft, shapeless body. The hanging flesh of her upper arms flapped when she gestured, and her fat gathered in folds over her dimpled elbows.

I was showing her a yoga pose I had learned. I wasn't athletic, I didn't dance or do sports, I wasn't good at most things physical, but I was flexible. I got her to sit in her living room chair, and I lay down on the carpet that stayed damp from the air conditioning she ran throughout the day and night. Once I saw she was focused on me, I raised my pelvis high. First, I did a bridge pose. Then, arching my back and lifting my hips even more, feeling space open up in my shoulders, I showed her my wheel pose. I stretched as far up as my body would go, my head hanging upside down so I could see the balcony behind me, my hands and feet planted firmly into the rug. I could tell I was steady, so for good measure I pushed my hips an inch higher and held my position for another breath. I exhaled and lay back on the rug. I stayed there with my legs folded under me, my arms at my sides. My grandmother didn't say anything. I wasn't sure if she had focused on what I had done. "Neat, right?" I asked her.

She had hardly nodded yes when with a serious expression she said, "You shouldn't do that around your father."

I was taken aback. Nobody had spoken to me like that. The idea that my father would not be able to handle my body surprised me, and I dismissed her comment. She didn't even know us. But maybe she was warning me because she knew firsthand that all kinds of things could happen to families. Her first husband, my Grandpa Sammy, had been inappropriate with his children and she herself had blurred boundaries, though not as extremely as Sammy. Maybe she worried that raising two daughters on his own would not be easy for my father.

This trip to see Grandma Doris and Grandpa Saul was a rare family vacation, as my mother gave little in child support and money was tight for my father. Grandma Doris had remarried after Grandpa Sammy left her for another woman. Despite his abuse and adultery, my grandmother begged Sammy not to leave her. She was ready to take him back which I find surprising because, for the most part, she was a formidable woman. She was outspoken, fairly cynical, and had a sharp sense of humor. Saul was much softer-spoken than Sammy and inclined, maybe even relieved, to let Grandma Doris take charge.

My father, Nava, and I spent mornings and evenings with her, but my father took us out to the swimming pool in the afternoons and let us try to play tennis on the building's courts. Nava, slimmer and more naturally muscular than I was, proved agile on the court, while I could not coordinate my big long limbs in any efficient way. My stomach spilling over the waistband of my, as usual, too-tight shorts, my long bangs flopping in my eyes, I approached each ball as if I were going to actually hit it. Each time I missed—and I missed almost every single ball—the momentum of my racket hitting only air set me off balance. I had no delusions that I was even remotely doing a good job, but I kept trying, hoping I'd get lucky or have a breakthrough. I lunged and righted myself, lunged and righted myself all over the court, with no idea of how to fix my approach or what exactly I was doing wrong.

~

Finally, it was the day we were going to Disneyland, the part of the trip we were most excited about. My father hated crowds and amusement parks so I imagine he was bracing himself when the three of us piled into the rental car to head to Anaheim. We didn't have a car in Queens; we walked or rode the subway. Driving was a novelty and an adventure. I liked moving through space with my family, my people, all of us packed up and snug, all going in the same direction at the same time.

Through my window the sky was whitish-gray that day, with bits of blue poking through, the road whipping by below me. Because I was in the front seat, I was in charge of air conditioning and music. I got to ride in front a lot of the time because my job was to help my father navigate. He called me Eagle Eye and told me I was good at keeping us headed in the right direction. Even though Nava got to sit up front sometimes, and he also told her she did a good job helping, I decided he was humoring her. I was the one who actually helped with the map, who engaged him in interesting conversation.

I rolled the dial on the radio to find a station that came in clear, stopping at whatever song sounded like pop. We were listening to "I Really Want to See You Tonight," by England Dan and John Ford Coley, when my father made a contented noise. A sort of "hmmmmmm," and he smiled.

"What is it?" I asked.

"The song, it's nice." I paid attention to the lyrics. "It's about a pretty night," my father said. "And the guy is singing about wanting to see someone. I don't know, it's nice."

I listened to the rest of the song without speaking. I wanted to better understand what the feeling of the song was about, to know more of what my father was trying to describe. I took it in, this male interpretation of romance and physical closeness, what it was to want love and to get it; I absorbed it as if I were made of clay.

When we stopped to get gas, the middle-aged white man behind the counter took notice of the three of us while we shopped for snacks. Knowing we had his attention I kicked our family repartee, especially my part in it, into high gear.

"Oh, Dad, can't we get some candy this once?" I asked as charmingly as I could, as if I were on a TV show about a single father and playing the role of easy-to-be-with-and-clever daughter.

"We don't need candy, we have fruit," he said.

"Sure, Dad, fruit is just like candy," I said rolling my eyes in an exaggerated way. Single-father families were rare and I did my part to spin our dynamic into something pleasing. My father liked being noticed by others, too. Raising my sister and me was a big part of his identity, something he knew he did well and something that set him apart. He wasn't just a divorced man; he was a man who could bring up two daughters by himself.

In the candy aisle my father, who never let us buy junk food except on the occasional sleepover we hosted, finally agreed to let my sister and me get some gum, and we brought a pack of Trident up to the cash register. The man behind the counter handed my father his carton of cigarettes. While my father fished out his wallet, the man, whose skin I now noticed had a gray tinge, gestured toward us and said, "It's sweet what you got here."

"Thank you." My father took the compliment with grace and didn't puff out about it the way he sometimes could.

"I have a daughter," the man said, looking down at my sister and me and back to my father. "We're not close anymore. I wish we were."

I searched his weathered face for more information, trying to uncover some clue as to why, wondering what could have happened. Was it his fault? Was he mean? He seemed harmless enough, but I knew there were many sides to a story. Was his daughter terrible? Or is that just how things went when you got older—you drifted away from your father? I could see that happening. Or, rather, I could see how that might have to happen, even to me.

The thoughts that came up from the man's comments were not new to me. I was beginning to feel a tug of concern—not fully conscious, still on the edge of my awareness—about how my father and I interacted. Hadn't Grandma Doris warned me not to do yoga poses in front of him? I wondered if the way our relationship functioned was acceptable. I felt warm and close with him, coy sometimes, the way daughters are, but our relationship was growing hazy at the edges, moving off into unknown territory where I couldn't see the boundaries. There wasn't a buffer there, a mother to keep it safe.

~

Near the end of our trip to California, the three of us went to Wet 'N' Wild water park, and I decided to wear my hair in two braids instead of down like usual. Most of the time I depended on a deep side part to keep only one eye visible, the other hidden behind the curtain of hair I left hanging; the school secretary that year called me Veronica Lake, a reference I didn't understand. Looking at myself in the hotel's bathroom mirror that morning, preparing for the water park, I announced to my father I was giving myself a little-kid hairstyle. I wanted to be just his daughter for the day, not try to be his equal or friend. What my grandmother said must have troubled me.

My father took a picture of me and Nava on a shaded bench when we first got to the park. In the photo, I'm leaning into her, and she is leaning into me, a long braid sprouting on either side of my head, and I'm beaming. That day I didn't worry about looking mature, and Nava and I played like sisters instead of me being in charge of her or acting like my father's confidant. We shot down water slides and leapt through the sparkling water, splashing each other, and I followed her into the ball pit so we could bury ourselves. I was one of the oldest kids in the fun zone area but I didn't care. I had never been to a place geared as much to children as this one.

At one point I looked back at my father, who sat nearby on a bench by himself, watching us, his face lost in thought, and I wondered if he was lonely. I thought about going over to him and keeping him company, to make sure he had fun too, but I pushed my worry aside and stayed in the water with my sister until it grew dark.

Gandhi's Lovely Assistant

Back in New York, the school year had started. I still had an enormous crush on Christopher Reeve, and Nava and I played dress up together now and then. When we played school, I was the teacher and she was the student; when we played castle, I was the queen, she the servant; and when we played house, I was the mom and she was the kid. Whatever the game, I was the authoritative woman who made Nava do my bidding and she complied. The only time I took orders from Nava was when she decided to be Gandhi, and I, stumped as to how I could adequately steal the focus from her, decided to give myself the role of Gandhi's lovely assistant, just like in a magic show.

In all things my priority was making myself attractive and experimenting with what kind of woman I could be. I wrapped one of my mother's old scarves from her time at the ashram around me into a makeshift sari and painted a bindi on my forehead in red lipstick. My sister turned on the new video camera our father had gotten for his public relations job at another Jewish nonprofit and Nava, who was adept at accents, knocked her impersonation of Gandhi out of the park. I didn't talk much as the assistant but smiled and mugged for the camera with my hands in prayer pose and tried to be charming.

When we played *Little House on the Prairie,* I was Ma and Nava was

Pa. I put on an ankle length hand-me-down skirt and pulled my hair up into a bun, and we sat in the clubhouse in our bedroom my father had built us out of wood. I popped up a small bowl of popcorn like they did on an episode we had just seen, and I took the filler that had fallen out from one of Nava's stuffed animals and worked it between two hairbrushes and pretended I was carding wool. By now we had adopted Sarah and Janine's ornery orange tabby, when they didn't want her anymore, and she sat with us inside. Nava and I did our best impressions of Michael Landon and Karen Grassle, respectively, from the TV show and I nodded my head and smiled sweetly the way Ma did to almost anything Nava-as-Pa said.

I was obsessed with Olivia Newton-John's album *Physical* and listened to it every day on our record player in the living room, until I knew the words to all the songs by heart. I had also seen an Olivia Newton-John special on TV featuring videos for almost every track on the album. My favorite was her animal rights song "The Promise" in which she swims and splashes with real live dolphins. I lay a blue-green bedsheet on our living room rug and set up the camera my father had for work on its tripod. I changed into my bathing suit, fluffed my hair out, pushed record, and spent that whole Saturday afternoon lip-syncing and rolling around the floor with imaginary dolphins.

~

Midway into my fifth-grade year my father began dating Celeste— the lovely, kind, generous, black-haired, Cuban-born woman at least ten years younger than he was. I can still see her dark brown eyes trained on my father, concentrating on what he was saying or disagreeing with it, her accent stretching her words into roller coaster rides of vowels and syllables, the ends of most of her sentences sounding like questions. The way she spoke made her seem playful, flexible. That's part of what I liked about her. She didn't need to be right or in control, she was happy simply to be with us.

"Hi, Celeste," I called when we came home late one Sunday afternoon from my mother's apartment, happy that she was there. Celeste walked in from the kitchen, wearing jeans and one of my father's flannel shirts with the sleeves rolled up. Her eyes lit up when she saw us. Nava gave her a hug. I'm surprised I wasn't annoyed when she wore his clothes, but any designs she might have had on my father didn't bother me. The apartment smelled good, and she told us she was cooking black bean soup. I dropped my weekend bag and sat on the couch with her. Nava brought her an armful of stuffed animals from our room, and Celeste hugged a worn bear to her face.

"What's his name again?" she asked, stroking his nubby fur.

"Honey," Nava said. "He's three."

"Oh, he's just a baby," she cooed and tucked him in her arms. Nava watched, pleased, squeezing the other animals to her chest. I curled my legs under me and settled deeper into the couch.

"How was the weekend?" she asked, turning to me, still speaking gently but moderating her tone, since I was two and half years older than Nava and in fifth grade.

"Good," I said, and leaned into her.

We were sitting there, quiet, Nava on Celeste's other side, when my father came in to ask if dinner was almost ready. Celeste got up, and I went into the kitchen after her to help serve the soup.

I think I would have been happy if she had married him. She didn't appear to worry about there being room for the two of us and her in his heart, and that endeared her to me. She seemed fond of me, and I was ready to invite her in. She didn't want to take my space, so I was glad to give her more of it.

One evening my father and I were talking in his office after Celeste had gone back to her apartment. They'd been together about six months by then. I was sitting in the secondhand upholstered chair he kept in the corner, and he had just finished smoking a cigarette. He sat perched on his dark to the right of his typewriter, his elbows resting on his knees. He wore a flannel shirt and jeans, his at-home clothes.

"How was your weekend?" I asked.

"Good."

"How are things with Celeste?" Nava and I liked her and we wondered if the relationship was getting serious.

"They're fine. But I think I'm going to break up with her."

"Really?" I'd be sorry to see her go, but his confiding in me made me feel important. "Why don't you like her?" I leaned toward him on the armrest so he could see I was interested.

"I like her," he said.

I nodded my head, signaling my ability to really listen, my readiness to understand.

"And the sex is good," he continued.

I flinched, unsure what to do with my face. I opened my eyes wider and tried to focus. He was entrusting me with his secrets, so I was willing to be his audience but I felt myself recoil.

I don't remember the next few minutes of conversation because I was concentrating so hard on trying to keep my face neutral. But my skin tingled and my head felt detached from my body as I left his office. If I had wanted to tell him I hoped he would keep dating Celeste, I couldn't now. He had taken her for himself; she no longer belonged to all of us. He had made her part of his other world. That sex world. The place I was beginning to both back away from and peer into—the one that would soon disturb the peace I'd found living with my father.

Boys and Wheels

Sometimes I still marvel that I got married. I had no blueprint for making a relationship work, and people in my family, at least in my parents' generation, split up all the time. My family—both sides—is riddled with men and women who never quite learned how to give all of themselves over to a partner and to trust that they themselves were lovable. I think both are necessary in order to build a healthy relationship and I spent my twenties and my thirties unable to do either.

It was in fifth grade when a boy expressed interest in me for the first time. We were at the skating rink where my mother had taken us one of the weekends she had us. I hadn't been on skates before but I didn't have to struggle too much to learn, which surprised me. I wasn't exactly coordinated but I took to it right away. My mother and Nava stayed together, Nava occasionally stumbling and falling, while I rolled along solo.

Having found my footing quickly, I soon picked up speed, allowing the music to move me, which was also surprising because of how I disliked dancing. Every time I maneuvered to pass through a slower group of skaters and didn't falter, I felt a thrill and went faster. Lights in the ceiling reflected off the shellacked floors in pink, green, red, and blue, bathing the other skaters' faces and bodies in otherworldly shades. I hoped I looked different under the lights too—maybe even beautiful.

During those few hours I felt a flicker of possibility. I, too, could be grown up and worldly like the teenagers doing laps around me. On the rink it was me leading, me controlling my direction for once. I skated laps and laps to Pat Benatar, Journey, and The Police, happy to blaze my own trail in an unspoken rhythm along with other skaters revolving around the center. I was on my own but surrounded, which seemed about the perfect scenario for me—neatly contained, moving fast, and independent of anyone else.

Girls clustered and skated together, while boys clumped up on the sidelines watching them or doing tricks in front of the girls they wanted to impress. I was glad I'd dressed up. I'd worn my better, tighter jeans and borrowed Nava's button-down pastel blouse with the glittery thread running through it and her polyester rose-colored vest trimmed in satin.

The fan's breeze blew through my hair as I curved with the arc of the rink, and the music the DJ played pulsed around me, through me. I felt my chest fill like a balloon inside my rib cage, ready to lift me up.

Then I spotted a cute boy my age who didn't look like the boys I went to school with. He was blond and so handsome he could have been on TV. When I passed him, I made sure my shoulders were back, my speed consistent. I thought he might be watching me and I smiled to myself. I skated well, allowing myself to take up more space on the rink. I could almost feel the me I wanted to believe was there but couldn't seem to get to, the one who was better than where I came from or who my parents were. One day soon I would no longer be a little girl who got shuffled around to different places, waiting on adults and reading faces. A girl you couldn't help but notice, who you could pick out from all the others because she was so special.

Every time I skated past the cute boy I grew more aware of him, until my focus was strictly about making sure he saw me. I didn't think about saying hello or even smiling at him. He probably had a house; he probably lived with both parents. He didn't know my uncle and his kids called me Miss Piggy and that I lived in Flushing with my father and roaches and that I safety-pinned the waistbands of my skirts together because they wouldn't close.

The DJ announced the next song would be a couples' skate, and I moved to the wall to exit off the rink as quickly as I could so I could sit it out. My hand was on the lip of the wall surrounding the rink, helping me to balance as I made my way to the carpeted bench area, when the blond boy skated up next to me. He had blue eyes, a kind face.

"Do you want to skate with me?"

I stared at him. No boy had ever approached me like this. I had not considered he would talk to me. I had never held a boy's hand.

My heart fluttering, I blurted out, "I have to leave now."

"Oh," he said, still looking at me. Then he glanced at the floor. "Okay."

"Thank you, though," I said, as if I was being offered a chair but preferred to stand. I skated past him to the benches and tried not to think about how nice he seemed.

I found my mother. "We have to get out of here."

"Why?" she asked. Nava was sitting next to her, sipping from a plastic cup.

"This boy asked me to skate with him. I told him we were leaving."

They watched me as I untied the thick brown laces of my rental skates.

"Are you sure you really want to leave?" my mother asked, glancing around the rink to find the boy who had asked me.

"Yes, let's go," I pleaded through clenched teeth without looking up in case he was nearby. I handed in my skates, grabbed my boots, and went to wait for my mother and Nava in the lobby, my heart pounding, my cheeks hot. Only when my mother and Nava joined me outside on the sidewalk and we had walked a block, squinting in the sunlight, did I begin to feel I could let my guard down.

Minutes later I felt the first twinges of regret for rushing away from the rink and the chance to spend time with this boy, but my need to protect myself was stronger. Maybe if I had said yes that day I could have chased away some of my fear. If I had let that boy take my hand and followed him back into the circle of bodies revolving around the center, I might have felt what it was like to trust that someone could like me.

This is how I would react to boys that were attracted to me from this point forward—never staying long enough for an actual connection to form, convinced that the fantasy version of me was better.

~

The next summer, when I liked another boy, this one at day camp, I was a little braver. Stefano was a year older than me, going into sixth grade, and tall, the tallest in our group, with dark hair and eyebrows and fair skin. Midway through our camp month, I told my friends I liked him. I rolled my denim shorts up higher, flipped my hair when I saw him, and when we lined up for our bus at the end of the day, I made sure to stand where I had the best chance of him noticing me. It was a game and I wanted to win. Days later, word got back to me that he wanted to "go out" with me. My friends were giddy. Stefano had told one of them he wanted to sit next to me on the bus ride back to Flushing at the end of our camp day.

Adrenaline pulsed through my body and made my arms weak. Heat rippled in my stomach. I managed to look excited but I was already plotting how to get out of the bus ride home with him.

I envisioned this boy sitting next to me. Talking to me. I would have to speak to him and I didn't know how to do that. What if he put his arm around me? I hadn't thought past the idea of winning his attention and now as much as I had wanted him to notice me is how badly I wanted him to forget about me.

The end of the day came and our camp groups lined up on the pavement in the hot afternoon sun. I was one of the tallest girls in my unit, so I hunched a bit and kept my head low. I didn't look around. I focused only on my friends' backs in front of me and tried to listen to what they were talking about, but I felt the weight of the situation pressing on me. As I stepped onto the bus, I fiddled with the hem of my T-shirt to avoid looking up, but from the corner of my eye I saw Stefano sitting by himself. I turned my head to look like I was talking to the friend behind me, and I walked down the aisle, past Stefano, to sit in the back.

The bus lumbered out of the campgrounds and onto the highway, with Stefano sitting by himself, me eight rows behind him, torn between relief at having gotten out of a bus ride with him and feeling awful for ignoring him. And for putting an end to a wish that had begun only a week ago.

Only two more weeks of camp were left. I said "hi" to Stefano when I was in a group and let him catch two hermit crabs for me when we took a camp day trip to Jones Beach, but I made sure I was never alone with him. The big kids had a special overnight to celebrate the end of camp and my friends joked about how Stefano and I would want to sleep near each other in our sleeping bags. I thought about his sleeping bag next to mine. I wondered if he would want to kiss me.

The night before the sleepover I lay in my bed at home and couldn't sleep. I felt as if a pit had opened up next to me and would swallow me if I didn't find a way to escape from the situation I had created. I couldn't figure out why I wasn't looking forward to spending time with the boy I supposedly liked, why his liking me didn't make me happy. What was the matter with me? Why, instead of excitement, did I only feel fear? Why, when I got what I was after, did I need to run from it? I had enjoyed Stefano's admiration from afar but now that he was getting closer, I had to escape.

I was afraid he'd want something from me that I couldn't give—afraid I would want something from him he wouldn't *want* to give. What started out feeling like my choice soon felt like someone else's demand. I didn't understand what I can see now, which is that I was learning about relationships from my father, who asked too much from me, and from my mother, whom I couldn't get enough of.

The next morning, I told my father I was sick. I faked a fever, putting my thermometer close to my light bulb when he left the room like I had seen Elliott do in the movie *E.T.* I knew I couldn't go on the overnight. At all costs, I had to stay home. And I did. My sister went to day camp, my father went to work, and I watched TV in my pajamas. I hunched over the coffee table in the living room, spooning corn flakes into my mouth, watching *Gilligan's Island* reruns. This was the real me, not the girl Stefano thought he liked.

Above the TV and on the wall across from the sofa hung scores of framed pictures Nava and I had drawn for our father. Picture after picture of girls and houses and girls with cats. Except for the occasional sun blazing high in the empty sky above them, the girls I drew stood alone on the page and had on lipstick and eye shadow. Their eyes were large and blue or sometimes green—never brown like mine—surrounded by long, thick lashes curled up high at the corners. Girls with ponytails, princesses with big heads and tiny necks in pink and lavender dresses with puffy sleeves. Because I wasn't good at drawing hands, I drew their arms behind their backs, where I imagined their invisible fingers were clasped. On the wall behind me, over the sofa, were the family photographs our father had also framed and hung. Baby photos, class photos, photos of Nava and me with our father, and of us with Aunt Ellen's daughters over the years. But no photos of our grandparents. None of our mother. None from our time on the kibbutz or Seattle. It was as if the three of us were on an island my father had sailed us to where we were safe from ashrams and Est; separate from the rest of the world and the way other people lived. We didn't have to compare our family to other families or feel what we were missing. On our island, everything was fine: we took care of each other and had everything we needed.

At lunchtime, I looked out the kitchen window and down at our building's swimming pool. Kids I didn't know splashed and screeched and the sun cut a triangle of light across the blue water, the remainder of the pool shaded by the next building over. I turned to the stove and heated a can of alphabet soup. In three hours, the babysitter would bring Nava home from camp. Counselors in my unit were probably passing out cold sandwiches and juice from black Hefty bags—a tablespoon of tuna fish in the middle of wheat bread, or globs of peanut butter and never enough jelly in the middle of white bread, and small cartons of thin, watery juice. The food wasn't good but it was ready for us precisely at noon; all I had to do was pick what I wanted. I liked sitting in a group in a field or in a clearing in the woods, eating with my friends and laughing, wondering what adventure the second half of the day would bring. The kibbutz part of me craved this routine and this extended family. I liked having so many people around me to choose from, I liked hiking and swimming in the chilly lake. I liked being away from the apartment. But now I was in hiding.

By the time fall came around it seemed like I couldn't hide even if I wanted to. I was in sixth grade and construction workers whistled at me when I passed. It happened often enough that when I got near a handful of guys in work helmets I felt my neck stiffen, my shoulders rise. I wondered if it was possible that by anticipating their scrutiny I was making them notice me in some way; I wondered if there was something about me that made them catcall. People told me I looked old for my age. Maybe some men assumed I was a teenager—though if they were looking closely enough, they would have seen I had no breasts and not much of a waist.

When guys in hardhats called out, "Yo, mami!" I wanted to yell back, "I'm not your mother!" But I didn't. I walked faster, knowing they were checking out my butt. I'd lower my backpack so they wouldn't get the chance to stare at my behind as I passed.

Sometimes, though, I didn't mind standing out. I was getting ready for bed one night in late August the summer I was almost twelve. The day had been muggy and the sun had gone down but it was still sticky out, the moisture in the air thick. I had brushed my hair and was braiding it to the side in front of my dresser mirror when I heard splashing from the pool downstairs. It closed at seven o'clock; it was now after nine. I went to my open bedroom window and looked out. There were two boys in the water, another climbing over the fence from the alley, and a fourth waiting for the last climber to get over the top and jump down. I figured they were my age, maybe a year or two older.

I watched the confident way they shrugged off their T-shirts and let those clothes drop to the cement that surrounded the pool. Their chests and arms and backs were tan, and their bodies were much more muscular than mine. One at a time, the boys plunged in. I gathered my baggy sleeping T-shirt closer around me and leaned on my windowsill to watch. They talked to each other in low voices, gliding from one side of the pool to the other as if they'd been in it before. Had they? I felt sneaky watching them—entering, it felt, where I didn't belong, witnessing their freedom. I wondered if they thought people in our building would see them at this hour. I wondered if they cared.

When one of them looked up and saw me, I felt my heart skip and almost ducked. But I also wanted to let them know they'd been discovered. I wanted them to discover me. I didn't move away.

The boy nudged one of his friends. That boy looked up and smiled at me. I waved.

Nava shuffled into our room holding a stuffed dog. "What are you doing?"

"Look," I told her, and motioned for her to come to the window where I had my forehead pressed against the screen.

She stood next to me clutching her dog. She peered out into the night and then caught movement from below. Two of the boys were swimming; the one who had smiled at me and another were still looking up at our window.

"They broke in," I told her, and waved once more.

"Don't!" she said, pulling my hand down.

I shook off her grip.

The boy who had smiled up at me first dove into the pool, surfaced, and looked up at me again. I smiled back at him.

"You should stop," Nava said.

I checked our bedroom door from over my shoulder. If my father came in from the other room, he wouldn't like it, but the situation was one I could manage: though I was letting myself wander into unexplored territory, I still felt safe. I was three stories up from the boys, they didn't know who I was, and I was partially in shadow. I was the one in charge, just the way I liked it.

The first boy got out of the water and stood across from my window. He gestured at me. I shrugged my shoulder and shook my head, indicating that I didn't understand. He gestured again, motioning that I should come down. I laughed a little. He did it again, and two of his friends got out of the water and joined him, all watching me.

"Come on," the first one called.

I didn't feel as anonymous as I had moments ago. I took a step back. "No," I mouthed and shook my head. Nava stood at my dresser, out of their sight but keeping an eye on me.

"Come down," the boy called again.

I looked at the ladder connected to the exterior wall of the building. I wondered if they could grab onto this fire escape on the first floor and climb up to mine if they wanted to. Suddenly, I didn't like that they knew where I lived.

"What's your name?" the first one called up. And then again, more loudly, "What's your name?"

"Nava, get the blinds on that side," I said. I reached for the cord to pull down the venetian blinds. My fingers fumbled; when I yanked, the blinds only half collapsed. I tried to steady my hands to grip the cord again. I pulled. Nothing happened. "Nava, get your side down!" I hissed. She was too slow. The boys were still looking up and watching. What if they climbed up after me? What if they scaled the fire escape while I was asleep and rapped on the window? What if they figured out what unit we lived in and found me in the lobby the next day?

"I'm going to tell Dad," Nava said.

I reset the cord and finally got the other side down. "Don't!" I snapped. "It's fine."

"Why did you do that?" she asked as I hurried past her on my way out of our bedroom and to the living room, where I knew I would feel safer.

I didn't answer. It was the first time I had pushed myself to see how far I would go and I was scared. Up to now, each time I had wanted a boy's attention, I'd gotten it. I liked having the spotlight on me, but I wanted to be able to shut it off and take cover whenever I chose. I had to be careful or I might create a situation for myself I couldn't handle.

The lights were on in the living room and the air conditioner hummed but my father wasn't there. I walked to the window and lowered those blinds too. I smoothed my hair and waited for my heartbeat to return to normal.

~

Around this same time my mother started seeing a new man. He had dull blond hair pushed away from his face and fair skin, but he wasn't bad looking. He came over on a weekend we were with her, and my mother went to the bathroom to do Nava's hair, leaving this guy and me alone in the living room. He was sitting on her royal blue velvet sofa, and I was sitting next to it on my mother's Persian rug. In the silence he made eye contact with me. I pressed my lips together. I didn't know what to say to him. It didn't occur to me that I didn't owe this stranger my interest, that I didn't owe him anything.

"You have luminous skin," he said.

I had heard the word before but hadn't used it myself. I knew it was a compliment meant for a woman. A grown-up compliment.

He leaned in close toward me, as if to confirm what he was noticing about me. "And your eyes are almond-shaped," he said.

I felt myself shrink but tried hard to keep my face still so he wouldn't think he had had an effect on me. I wish now I had had the courage then to stare him down. I wish I could have been the kind of girl who thought to yell out, "Mom, guess what your creepy boyfriend just said to me?"

But at the time I wasn't absolutely sure that what he was doing was bad. It was definitely not a normal thing to say, but I couldn't identify what was troubling me. The words weren't wrong; it was the intensity with which he spoke them and how he looked at me that was, the way he was noticing me and that he said these things only after my mother had left the room.

After another moment of his eyes on me I got up to find my mother. I stood in the doorway of the bathroom where she was finishing Nava's hair. If she had looked over at me or checked in with me, it's possible I would have let her know I wasn't comfortable, but she didn't, and I didn't say anything to her. I didn't want to make her feel bad that he had given me such a compliment when she was the one he was dating and I didn't want to complicate any part of my relationship with her.

I never saw him again nor did I ask my mother what had happened to him. Like most things, I tried to push it as far away from my mind as I could.

That was the summer the world unfolded into a more dangerous place, one with borders I could not find and rules I didn't always understand, a more grown up version of the world I had been living in all this time. People paid attention to me now, the way I'd always craved, but they were the wrong people and they paid attention for the wrong reasons.

One Saturday night Nava and I were with our mother, crossing Seventh Avenue to get to Penn Station. I looked over to see a tall man, probably in his forties, leering at me over the heads of the people between us. My body knew what he was after before my mind did, and in that instant I understood in my bones, in my blood, that I was being eyed like prey. This was different from the "yo, mami" construction men. There was something almost playful about those guys compared to the way this man had trapped me in his stare. I was barely twelve. I wondered if he had picked me because I sent out signals without realizing it. Could he tell in a subliminal way that I wanted attention, that I wasn't an innocent girl? That from my bedroom window I had teased boys down in the pool, that I flipped through my father's dirty magazines when he was at work?

I broke the man's stare and moved closer to my mother. I realized there was no way for me to stop what was happening, for me to keep men from noticing me, from invading my space. I couldn't go back to being a kid even if I wanted to.

Lady of the House

On the weekends my father had us, we went on errands to the bank and hardware store and rummaged through garage sales, picking up another bookshelf or lamp or toy. On a Friday or Saturday night every week or two, depending on money, my father might take us out to dinner at our favorite Chinese restaurant, Lychee Village, which I loved because I didn't have to cook. We ordered pizza in once a week or so but eating out was my favorite. No clean up, no dishes. People-watching and a Shirley Temple with extra cherries.

During those dinners out, when we were on our extra good behavior, my father was more charming and less weary. One night after we ordered I finished my story about a boy I liked named Derrick and then Nava mimicked me in a Brooklyn accent. My father laughed and his eyes glimmered. When I came back from taking Nava to the restroom, he watched us with a look I recognized, one that made me change my behavior; my walk back to the table became a promenade because I could see him welling with pride. "I like seeing you take care of each other. I'm a lucky dad," he said.

We were his emissaries in the world, proof that he was doing a good job. One of his nicknames for me was "Pretty" and he'd sometimes say women wanted to date him "because they can see what beautiful babies I make." Back then I didn't mind him basking in me, taking inventory of who I was to him and assessing me. The feeling of being seen and valued by a parent whose opinion I prized was intoxicating.

When we still lived in Seattle and my parents were newly separated, my father took me out on what he called "dates" canoeing and to movies. Now, on the night of my first "date" in seven years with him alone, I kissed Nava goodnight and waved goodbye to the babysitter, as if I was a mother leaving the apartment with my partner headed out for a night of fun. My arm looped in my father's, I gallivanted down Kissena Boulevard like I had won a prize. I felt protected and, most importantly for me, chosen. We went to dinner and I told him about my day at school and who was fighting with whom and what girl had done what. I reveled in our father-daughter time and came home that night rejuvenated.

On a date several months after that, I decided to wear my father's ivory Irish sweater, his fisherman's cap, and his coat, an army-surplus bomber jacket in military green. They were all big on me but I didn't care. They were proof of our connection. We headed down Kissena again and I took his arm. "Aw, I like that," he said.

It was cold and dark out, the shops still open but closing soon. We went to Lychee Village, the way we always did, but ate more quickly, since we had a movie to catch. Even though it was rated R, I had convinced my father he should take me to *Christine,* the latest movie adapted from a novel by Stephen King.

The theatre was an old one, with ornate carvings and moldings in the lobby from a time when Flushing was a part of the promise of New York City. It must have been beautiful when it was built, but was run down now. A paint-chipped balcony looked over the worn, red velvet seats below. Heavy beige curtains hung in front of the screen and, when the lights dimmed, they dragged opened in slow motion, like somebody had grown tired while pulling the cord.

My father and I bought popcorn and Coke and found seats. I chatted and watched other people file in. The theatre filled with the sounds of couples settling into their seats, their muffled laughs and whispers, the scent of perfume and minty gum.

In the dim theatre with my father, surrounded by adults on dates, part of me grew alert, uneasy. Maybe it wasn't clear anymore that I was his daughter; maybe those around me would mistake me for my father's young girlfriend. I hoped I still looked enough like a kid that I wouldn't give anyone the wrong impression. For good measure, I called him "Dad" several times as I talked to him, spackling the awkwardness with words, as I tended to when I was self-conscious. My father leaned toward me and listened while I stammered and then grew quiet. I was thankful when the movie started and I could look at the screen without thinking.

The suspense and gore made the film scarier than I had anticipated, but that didn't bother me as much as the lust between the men and women on screen. Every time the characters started fooling around, I braced myself. The two leads made out and I pulled to the left of my father so that our shoulders couldn't touch. I wanted to get out of there. Though I had picked the movie, I wished we hadn't come.

But I didn't want to admit what was wrong. He was the parent I was most connected to, and if I told him how I was feeling, our bond could become tenuous, our relationship awkward. Besides, what kind of girl became uncomfortable around her father unless something was wrong with her? I had no courage to acknowledge my uneasiness and no language to express it. Instead of saying, "This movie is a gross one to watch with you, Dad. Let's go home," I hunkered down and fortified myself. My father, for his part, didn't say or do anything to indicate he was troubled or that we should leave, and so we stayed.

My new discomfort with our closeness surprised me because in other ways I'd only grown bolder. I'd been snooping in his bedroom for the last year. Nava and I were often on the hunt, but I was more driven. Sometimes after school I brought friends over—mostly my best friend Claudia and the same friends who helped me crank call sex lines to mess with the women on the other end—and I took them into his room with me.

My father had a pretty hefty collection of *Playboy* magazines.

(Strangely, Grandpa Sammy had passed them along to him before leaving for Florida.) My father also had magazines entitled *Oui*. Still a year away from taking French class in middle school, I could not imagine what "oui" meant or how to say it. In my head I pronounced it "ow-ee," which I thought might refer to the discomfort the ladies in the magazine appeared to experience with sex, their eyes shut and heads thrown back, with wincing glossy mouths, or their eyebrows arched high in surprise over vacant-looking eyes, and open, pouting lips.

I'd pick out a magazine from the stack on his bathroom floor. Crouching on the tile I studied each photo, only turning the page when I had taken in everything I could about the model: her eye color, lipstick, jewelry, and hair. I scrutinized her body, wondering if I would grow up to look like that too, if I would ever do the things she was doing in that photo.

Once, I stole enough quarters from the laundry-money mug in my father's room to purchase a copy of *Playgirl*. Claudia was with me when I bought it at a mom-and-pop corner store we didn't usually go to. I tossed the magazine on the counter as casually as I could and the cashier stared at me for a long moment. I wasn't sure she'd sell it to me but then she accepted the quarters I counted out, and I snuck the magazine home in my bag. We looked at it for a little while but the photos of naked men didn't enthrall me the way I had hoped.

I threw the *Playgirl* out and went back to snooping in my father's drawers. It didn't occur to me that it was reasonable for a parent not to reveal everything to their kids. For me, anything he kept private signaled an unsettling distance between us, an omission or a breach of trust. If Nava and I were indeed my father's primary focus, if we three were a family and I was his partner, there was no reason for him to keep himself apart from us.

I didn't understand why there had to be a dividing line between our family of three and his private romantic life, why he needed a space for himself. Especially because he was so open with us in other ways. When he and Nava and I ran errands in the neighborhood on weekends, I saw him notice the women we walked by, and whenever Nava and I watched TV with him and a pretty woman came on, he snapped to attention. "Hello there," he'd say, or, "Who do we have here?" as if the woman had appeared on screen just for him. I took note and assessed her, too, searching for what made her so special, and how I might be captivating in that way.

On an afternoon when Nava was at a friend's house and my father was at work, I went into his room again. Since he'd quit cigarettes and started smoking a pipe, the cooped-up air in there smelled more like fresh cut tobacco and apples than ash. He'd slice up a Red Delicious or Macintosh and let Nava and me sprinkle small, pale chunks of the fruit into his Captain Black because he'd heard it kept the tobacco moist.

I scanned his bathroom and rifled through his desk drawer. I moved to his bedroom closet and opened the accordion doors. I studied his shoes, checked his shelves. I flipped through his dress shirts, smelling each one for perfume, hoping I could unearth the hidden partners in my father's life, looking for a sign of the women I was certain he'd had over but didn't know about. Toward the end of his rack of starched shirts, I found what I was looking for—evidence that he had a secret, someone who belonged only to him, separate from me. This shirt was collarless and sheer; it looked like a woman's nightshirt.

I took the nightshirt off the hanger, stripped to my underwear, and slipped the shirt on. I stood on his bed so I could check myself out in the mirror that hung on the opposite wall. I flipped my hair and stuck my hips to one side with the confidence I had seen in women who acted sexy. I struck the poses on my father's old matchbook covers. I worked my face into expressions like those I had seen in his magazines: the pained looks of ecstasy, the fake shyness. I flipped my hair again and pouted. I wanted to see if I measured up to his girlfriends. I knew I could be grown-up in this way, too.

Then, almost like a gear inside me had ratcheted too far, nausea washed over me. My mouth went dry. I knew with every part of me that what I was doing was wrong, that I didn't want this.

I flung the shirt off of me, fumbled it onto its hanger and slammed his closet doors shut. Clutching my clothes, I hurried out of his room, away from his private life and the things that went on in there that I wasn't supposed to be part of.

From there on out, I kept myself as far away from him, emotionally and physically, as I could. I never drank from his water glass, never borrowed his jacket or hat again for fear it would magically bind us. Any way I could keep us apart, I did.

As I left childhood, I invented more rituals that I believed prevented our closeness. I didn't taste anything from his plate or fork and when I did laundry for the household after school every Friday, I washed my father's and Nava's clothes together, and mine and Nava's together, but would not mix mine with his. And when we walked in the neighborhood, I stayed far ahead of him and Nava or lagged behind, hoping I could break off from their family of two and protect myself from playing the pseudo-mom, the pseudo-partner role I'd grown so uncomfortable with. My father would ask Nava why I was so angry with him and she tried to explain, but she didn't understand it. I didn't fully understand it either.

I see now that because my father was unaware of or unable to see the natural separation adolescents go through with their parents, I was driven to create a rift between us, a kind of moat that he wouldn't dare cross. If he wasn't going to give me the space I needed, I would distance myself. I no longer wanted the power in the house, I didn't want to be grown up or pretty around him. I wore baggy clothes, stopped casually chatting with him and removed any enthusiastic inflection from my voice when we did speak. The closeness I'd had with him, the way he'd treated me like a grown up, when I was too young to really understand what that meant, had now become something dangerous, like the boys in the pool knowing where I lived.

I began to use Nava as a buffer since she had been, and still was, the bona fide child in the family. Certainly, she was far more innocent than I was, incapable of making incorrect, inappropriate decisions as I had, like going on dates with my father and wearing his clothes. It was, I felt, my fault that my father and I had been too close. It never occurred to me that he might need to also consider our boundaries; that maybe he could have provided a different structure to our home life so I could stop taking on the role of his partner, our mainly-missing mother.

Karma's a Bitch

When I think about the last weekends we spent with my mother in the city I think of her homemade lasagna, walking everywhere, and the movies she took us to, like *Raiders of the Lost Ark*, *Starman*, and *Terms of Endearment*, which was the first movie that made me cry. My throat tight, my nose running, I tried to dab my eyes dry in the dark as nonchalantly as I could, so she and Nava wouldn't see. I was embarrassed that a movie had gutted me. I didn't yet understand why a fictional story of a mother and daughter's tumultuous and ultimately loving relationship had left me wrecked.

One Saturday my mother took us bike riding for the first time, renting bicycles near the East River where we could practice on the long, winding, wide path that ran along the water. Our father didn't want to get us bikes. He didn't even want to teach us how to ride. The several times we had asked, he said he was afraid we'd go too far and accidentally wander into the unsafe areas of Flushing. So my mother used one of her weekends to introduce us to something new, the way she had with roller-skating.

I don't remember the learning part, only the hours of cycling afterward: the trees and people blowing by, the power I felt in being able to move as fast as I wanted. I rarely spent time in parks and never went hiking or traveled to new places like other kids my age seemed to. For the most part, my scenery never changed; apart from time in the summer at camp, city living was all I knew.

From where we cycled along the East River, I could look across and see Brooklyn, where two of my cousins lived with Uncle Bobby—the Miss Piggy Uncle—and Queens, where my father would be waiting for us in our quiet apartment when we got back home on Sunday. I pedaled harder and allowed myself to forget about them.

With the river on one side and my sister and mother on the other, I traveled away from the confines of my life, fast. I was uncatchable.

I could see a glint of who I would become, the distances I could go when I was no longer stuck in my Flushing childhood. Did my mother know she was offering me this kind of freedom? Maybe this is how she'd felt when she moved to Israel, left for India, left my father, or dropped Nava and me off on Sunday nights.

I loved my body moving at high-speed, the wind against my face and through my hair, my heart pounding in my chest. I had not felt this lightness, this kind of abandon, with my father. Perhaps when I was a toddler on the kibbutz and he took me swimming, but not for years and years. In fact, over the last year my father had become cranky and irritated more and more of the time. Being around him felt bad, like wearing a scratchy sweater, like having tired, burning eyes. I remember thinking he must be sexually frustrated, but I don't recall where I had heard the term or how I knew it. His irritation seemed to bubble and seethe, his energy was jagged and angry, and his feelings escalated quickly. He had punched a hole in my bedroom door and had cracked a dustpan into several pieces when he threw it across the kitchen. He'd never hit me, but there was a palpable level of rage inside of him.

Even before this period with my father, I had always believed something was missing with him, and it was not his fault. How could he compare with my mother? She didn't provide for our day-to-day needs, but she was the one I wanted. Being with my mother was like breathing again, being with my source. I belonged to her before I belonged to anyone else. She gave us experiences and freedom. She was the gift parent, the one who showed me new places, who fed me new foods, who I could be a girl around, and then later, a teenager comfortable with my changing body in a way I never was and would never be around my father.

~

I was twelve years old and over the last several months Nava, my mother, and I had started talking about us living with her again sometime soon. My mother said she was thinking of getting a farm upstate where the three of us would be together, have a couple of dogs and some cats and a garden and a cow. But then she stopped talking about a farm and said just a regular house upstate would be better. Shortly after that she told us that renting an apartment was more practical and even took Nava to look at one with her in Queens. I let myself imagine what our life would be like—waking up with her there every morning, seeing her after school each day and having dinner together every night. It was what I had wanted for as long as we'd been apart. She had always felt out of reach and soon, though I didn't know it yet, she would be gone again.

On a Saturday night in early June, Nava and I were on our way to a restaurant with her when she said she wanted us to meet somebody, a new friend she'd made named Karma.

"Karma," I said. "What kind of name is that? What does it mean?"

"It means destiny," my mother said, still walking and looking ahead.

Karma was already at a table when we got there. A tall woman with fair skin and fluffy, light brown, shoulder-length hair, she smiled in a way I didn't like, and though I didn't realize why at the time, she had a familiar presence. She spoke to me from a remove, sitting back in her metal chair with her puffy halo of hair. There was a stillness to her, and she was watchful, as if she were assessing me. Maybe I was on edge because I knew to be wary of new people my mother brought into her life—like boyfriends and spiritual leaders. Or maybe my intuition was that good. Part of me already knew my mother's judgment was suspect and Karma struck me as fake, like she was hiding something.

"Ronit has a show coming up at school. She loves to sing," my mother said, trying to fill the silence at the table.

"Oh?" Karma said nodding her head in my direction.

"Yep," I said taking a sip of ice water. "I'm Rizzo in *Grease*."

"Hmm," she said with the same static smile stuck to her face, her eyes drifting to passersby.

Our dinner went on in much the same way, with Karma reclining in her chair and reacting to what the rest of us talked about but not saying much. I kept my eye on her.

Couples and people walking alone passed by on the other side of the restaurant's roped off area separating diners from foot traffic. My mother leaned over and moved Nava's hair from where it was still tucked into the back of her T-shirt and Nava giggled.

"That tickles," she said, hiking her shoulders up.

"Do you want me to play with your hair?" Karma asked.

"Yes!" Nava said, her big green eyes twinkling.

"Scoot your chair over," Karma said.

Nava moved closer to her and Karma began smoothing back her hair and massaging her head. Nava closed her eyes and tilted her head forward.

I couldn't believe Nava wanted this weirdo touching her—didn't she see what I saw? I looked at my mother. She seemed to be fine too. What was wrong with everyone? I didn't know exactly what Karma was up to but I was on guard from the beginning.

Did I sense my mother was making plans without Nava and me? Or did I simply dislike the intrusion this woman posed. Whatever it was, the next day my mother revealed that Karma was involved with Bhagwan. The disinterested smile on her face when she'd sat with Nava and me made sense then. I had seen that smile back in Seattle at the Rajneeshee center when I was five years old. It reminded me that when it came to my mother, I couldn't ever be sure what was about to happen, that she was uniquely capable of disrupting my world.

I could think of only one time when I had liked how she surprised me. A couple of years earlier, she told us to pack something nice in our overnight bags because we had a special plan on Saturday night. When she picked us up on Friday, she wouldn't tell us where we were going that weekend. By early Saturday evening when she and Nava and I headed toward midtown together—me wearing my favorite black dress with pink flowers and a ruffle on the bottom, white tights, and patent leather shoes—she still wouldn't say.

We walked to 49th Street, then 52nd, Nava and I continuing to guess what it was we were doing. My mind zigged and zagged, trying to figure it out. I kept asking my mother where we were headed and she kept saying, "Hmmm…I don't know." I hadn't seen my mother act playful like that before. I hoped the surprise was good. I believed it was, but I wasn't ruling out that it was something I didn't actually want to do, like going to one of her parties or visiting one of her friends.

At 52nd Street, she stopped and told us we were waiting for someone. Nava and I kept asking her questions, and my mother looked like she was trying to hold back a smile. The less she said, the more incredible I imagined the surprise was. I thought maybe she was getting married and wanted to introduce him to us. Maybe we were going on a trip together. Or, I thought, the closer we got to midtown and the theatre district, maybe I was going to finally see my favorite star, Christopher Reeve in person. Only a year or two had passed since I sent off my fan letter soaked in the tears I'd shed out of my desperation to meet him.

We stood back from the street near a brick building. Taxicabs clogged the road and honked, their headlights glowing brighter and brighter in the darkening night. The smell of hot pretzels and hot dogs from the carts near us wafted by in the chilly air. Adults and a few families passed us on their way to different Broadway shows. Lots of little girls and their mothers walked into the Alvin Theatre twenty feet away, whose marquees advertised the musical *Annie*.

After we had waited about five minutes, my incessant, "What is it? What is it?" punctuating the time, my mother looked at Nava and me and said, "Oh, well, we might as well see *Annie*."

Nava and I stood there looking at her.

"Come on," she said, "let's go in!" and she led the way.

I had never been to a show with my mother, only with my father and Nava once, and one time with Tracy. I followed my mother as she wove her way into the lobby. This was really happening. A true, good surprise with no complications. But it was only after we'd moved past the throngs crowding the concession and souvenir stands and made it to our assigned aisle, that I began to believe there wasn't any part of the plan I needed to second guess.

My mother sat between Nava and me and I marveled at the velvet seats, the ornate proscenium, the twinkling chandeliers in the impossibly high ceiling. I was flipping through the program when the lights went down. The overture played and when it ended Annie's voice rung out through the theatre. I hadn't heard someone young sing like that, with a voice so strong and certain. Soon the rest of the orphans romped across the stage, their voices blending and rising together. My mouth agape, goosebumps running down my arms, I could think of nothing better than this. It was as if the cells of my body were vibrating, my insides stirred up and buzzing from the sounds pouring over me from these actresses—these girls my age.

That night I realized I wanted to be like them. I wanted to not only be in school choruses but sing leading roles in musicals. I wondered how my voice compared to theirs, if I could ever have enough of what it took to make it. I wasn't jealous exactly, but enthralled and aching to do what they did. To mesmerize an audience with my talent and to be seen. To be surrounded by castmates—friends, even—performing together on stage night after night only pretending to be orphaned, in real life far from forsaken. In real life a star.

I didn't question my mother's choice of shows, the fact that *Annie* might be a painful story for me and Nava. All that mattered was the happy ending. Watching this performance, I was the most content I could recall having ever been. My mother had thought of us, known what we would like, and had gone ahead and organized this night for us. This was what I wanted above all else, the story I wanted to tell myself more than anything: that my mother loved us so much she was happy to arrange her life around Nava and me.

But now, two years later, she was leaving. I have no memory of whether or not she did this on the phone or in person, but a few weeks after we met Karma, just before Nava and I left for sleepaway camp, my mother told us she was going out for a few weeks to Rancho Rajneesh, the 64,000-acre ranch Bhagwan had established in Antelope, Oregon. She said she'd be back by midsummer. I wonder if she knew then she'd be gone longer than that. I don't know how much she lied to herself and how much she lied to us.

I blamed Karma. If she hadn't come into my mother's life and reminded her about Bhagwan, she wouldn't have wanted to leave us. Once again, I didn't hold my mother responsible.

For many years I wanted to believe my relationship with my mother was like that of most kids, just broken up into weekends. I didn't want to acknowledge the obvious, that I was growing up without her. I don't think I could have tolerated knowing my sister and I would never be enough to keep her rooted.

Bhagwan Returns

I was an adult when I learned that Bhagwan not only encouraged sannyasins to lead celebratory lifestyles but was often referred to as "the sex guru." The foundation of his philosophy was that sexual repression was the root of most psychological problems and he believed monogamous marriage was unnatural. He prescribed sex as the antidote and promoted unrestricted promiscuity among his sannyasins, in addition to partner-swapping, from the age of fourteen.

In his book *The God That Failed,* Hugh Milne, a former bodyguard of Bhagwan's, describes, "frequent changes of partner among ashram members. This, plus our own inclinations, engendered an atmosphere of frank promiscuity, a promiscuity for which the ashram was already becoming famous in the outside world." According to Milne, the ashram was home to sexual feasts, "the likes of which had probably not been seen since the days of Roman bacchanalia."

The disinterested look in the sannyasin's eyes I saw when I was five at those early meditations with my mother in Seattle, and also with Karma in the city at dinner, made even more sense now. Kids were not only distracting to their parents and a hindrance to spirituality; they were a downright obstacle to living the sensual and free-love life Bhagwan promoted and expected. "The nuclear family is a disease," Bhagwan preached. He needed his followers to focus on him, not their own offspring or loved ones.

He lectured that only some women were ready to bear children, that most needed their energy for personal growth. In my opinion it's maintaining one's patience and respect even when children won't sleep, won't listen, and become generally challenging that's evidence of real growth. It's so much easier to work on yourself when you're alone, so much less demanding to have a one-sided conversation. Actual growth comes from learning how to sustain an honest and emotionally intimate relationship with others.

In 1981, two years before my mother went to Rancho Rajneesh, Bhagwan arrived in New Jersey. According to Milne, upon exiting his plane Bhagwan paused at the top of the stairs and "the sage expansively proclaimed: I am the Messiah America has been waiting for." Bhagwan had fled India with millions of dollars in unpaid taxes and other legal troubles hounding him.

The next year Bhagwan moved operations to 64,229 acres in Central Oregon on a property knows as the Big Muddy Ranch, near Antelope, Oregon. Bhagwan's mostly Western followers had raised millions of dollars in donations to fund their new sprawling community. On Rancho Rajneesh in their new city of Rajneeshpuram, sannyasins established a metro system, a strip mall, the 145-room Hotel Rajneesh, a post office, fire department and police, a medical clinic and their own airstrip. They worked long hours to keep the commune going—digging, building, farming, and serving Bhagwan and his right-hand woman, Ma Anand Sheela. At its height, 7,000 red- and orange-clad sannyasins lived on the property.

The Netflix docuseries *Wild Wild Country* provides ample footage of both the Pune ashram and of Rancho Rajneesh in Oregon—they had plenty of it to draw from, because the Rajneeshees believed they were building a civilization for the ages and documented most everything. In frame after frame, sannyasins dance in their red and orange clothing and their black-beaded malas, their arms flung in the air, their hands shaking like Aspen leaves in a squall—hundreds of them jumping wildly, seemingly in ecstasy until they collapse to the ground, utterly spent.

Bhagwan offered his followers the sense that they were truly special, that they were spiritually elevated, and they believed it. And it is true that my mother looked beautiful when she came back from her ten months on the ashram in India, as if she were lit up from the inside—almost proof that she was on a transcendent path. I always disliked when she shared Bhagwan's quotes with us, but what really got under my skin was when she said his name with the emphasis on the second syllable: BhagWAN. I suppose this made her pronunciation more authentic but to me it was a sign she'd dropped further down the rabbit hole. Whether she meant to do it or not, her saying his name that way further separated her life from mine.

Bhagwan lectured in Oregon far less than when he was in Pune and then went into a silent period. Regardless, most days he did deign to drive by slowly in one of his ninety plus Rolls Royces and wave at his sannyasins, who lined the road to catch a glimpse of their leader and shower his car with flowers. The ranch was the iteration of the ashram Bhagwan and his close associates envisioned would be their headquarters for a world takeover. Bhagwan and Ma Anand Sheela had big plans, including overseeing research in several Rajneeshpuram labs where scientist sannyasins were, among other things, developing salmonella and working on isolating and possibly weaponizing the HIV virus.

When I watched *Wild Wild Country* I kept looking for my mother, zeroing in as quickly as I could on the throng of mostly Caucasian faces, often rewinding the program to scan the dark-haired women. I wanted to see her on the screen and at the same time I didn't. I don't know how I would have felt to discover her among the dancers or meditators or menial laborers on the ranch. But then, when I couldn't find her, I was disappointed. Maybe I wanted proof that she was there and happy, that it had been worth being away from us. Maybe I didn't.

I also looked for children or even teenagers in the footage, but the filmmakers didn't spend time on them. I wanted to catch a glimpse of their experience growing up on the ranch. I wondered how disrupted my life would have been if my mother had taken us with her to the ashram in India or even Oregon.

In *The Rajneesh Chronicles,* Win McCormack, who covered Rajneesh for *Oregon Magazine* from 1983-1986, interviewed a social worker sannyasin from the ranch who said that in her opinion there was a, "tremendous amount of child neglect going on at Rajneeshpuram." She described children as being, "one of the lowest priorities of any concern," and, "given very little attention." She noted too that most of the, "twelve-, thirteen-, and fourteen-year-old girls at the ranch were having sexual relationships," some with adults.

In one of his more recent essays, "Outside the Limits of the Human Imagination," published in *The New Republic,* McCormick writes that, "of all the reprehensible aspects of the Rajneesh cult, the treatment of children at the ranch has been the most ignored or suppressed, probably because it is the most horrible and painful to contemplate." Accounts include unsupervised children, injuries to children left to wander freely on the property, children rarely seeing their parents, over-sexualized children exposed to their parents' and other adults' sexual encounters, and older men paired with young teenage girls.

There are those who will tell you that within Bhagwan's teachings of liberation, it wasn't child abuse to let the kids there, "choose their own path." There are those too, like Ma Anand Sheela, who seem to assert to this day that martial law on the ranch was necessary, and she and her minions were justified in developing and planning to use biological weapons in order to liberate the world from outdated social structures—that in the end, they'd bring higher consciousness to the world.

It's hard to see how any rational adult would buy such a claim, but in some ways, it doesn't matter if I believe in what Bhagwan was selling or what he stood for. I can believe in people believing him. I can't fault someone for falling for a person or an idea that made them feel safe and loved. I understand safe. I understand the desire to belong. Don't we all want to know we are accepted and secure? If you feel untethered it can be hard to make good choices. What my mother wanted from the ashram is what I wanted from her. I believed in her, she believed in Bhagwan. We both lost.

End of a Long Run

I plopped myself onto the scraggly grass, avoiding the daddy longlegs. It was summer 1985, a few months before I turned thirteen, and Nava and I were away at a no-frills Jewish sleepaway camp. The upstate-New York compound was in the woods and had latrines instead of toilets, and no screens or glass on the cabin windows, just tarps that lowered at night. My mother had left for Rancho Rajneesh a few weeks before.

We were halfway through our six-week stay when the camp director arranged for us to listen to a guest speaker talk to our group about cults. My cabin-mates and I had left our regularly scheduled arts and crafts hour to gather in a clearing between the dining hall and the path to the lake. A worn, split-rail fence separated the paved camp road from the clearing, but we were not allowed to sit on it. Nava sat up front with the other ten-year-olds in her group. I sat on the grass next to my friend Josie—who, like me, did not have clothes as cool as those of the other girls in our bunk—and tried to fix my socks again.

The other girls had thick, scrunchy socks that were puffy at the ankles and came in lots of colors that coordinated with their outfits, but I didn't. Our father bought us most of our T-shirts and shorts at Modell's, the discount sporting goods store on Main Street. Despite having only boys' stretched-out cotton T-shirts and about three pairs of shorts, what I fixated on was the issue of my socks. I must have decided it was the only area of fashion where I had a chance to compete.

Every morning I put on two pairs of boys Modell's white tube socks. Though I carefully folded and scrunched the first pair around my ankles and then folded and scrunched the second pair over them, I didn't achieve the volume around my ankles I hoped for. Wearing two pairs of socks also made my shoes too tight. But I persisted throughout the summer, fussing, as I did now, with my socks, trying to plump the thin worn cotton into fullness.

I looked up from my ankles and sized up the skinny, unassuming bearded man waiting for us to settle down. He said he'd been asked to speak to us about the dangers of being swept away by one of the many cults in the world and began to review the warning signs of cult-like organizations.

"Whether a cult leader is living or dead," he said, "cult members show them absolute devotion. The cult leader's thoughts, opinions, and belief system are considered absolute truth. Another sign is if the group separates itself from the rest of the world. This can mean in the way they think and behave, but most of the time the group will be actually separate from the rest of the world physically."

As I listened, I began to feel a kind of heat spread across the right side of my head. The roots of my hair tingled, like feathers were tickling my scalp. I felt lightheaded, as if a part of me had drifted away.

"Most cults ask their followers to cut out contact with their family and friends. Friends and family members might notice," he went on, "that they never seem to see their loved one anymore because being in a cult means their contact with outsiders is extremely minimal. It could even be as drastic as choosing to live among members."

I listened along with the other kids but felt as if I had cartoon arrows pointing at my head, and everyone was staring at me. When he asked if anyone had questions, I didn't raise my hand but when the talk was over my cabin mates pushed me forward before the counselors took them to their next activities. I don't remember how they knew about my mother, when exactly I had told them about her that summer. But I'm sure I'd turned it into an off-the-cuff remark in an effort to seem worldlier than them. They might have expensive United Colors of Benetton T-shirts and matching socks, but I knew I had them beat in the interesting life department.

Nava's counselor had brought her to me and we stood with the man next to the fence.

"I hear your mother is on a commune," he said, his brown eyes searching our faces.

"She's in Oregon with Bhagwan Shree Rajneesh," I told him in the casual way I had perfected, still undecided about what direction to take while talking to this man. Should I play the girl who was unflappable and fine, or the one whose mother had left her yet again?

"What do you know about Bhagwan?" he asked in a kind voice.

"His followers have to wear sunset colors and a beaded necklace with his face on it," I said rolling my eyes like it was all so dopey. "She followed him to India too. But we live with our father."

"She went to Oregon last month," Nava said.

"That's serious," he said. "Rajneeshpuram—what Bhagwan is leading—is a cult."

I wanted to hold up a shield to protect us, to fling what he was saying off us. I didn't need this information. I didn't want it.

Nava started crying.

I felt tears but I willed them not to drop.

"I don't know. I'm not sure…" I said, backing away from him a bit.

"It absolutely is a dangerous cult."

He tried to talk with us a little more but soon our counselors came and took us to rejoin our groups.

"It's okay," I told Nava, wiping her cheeks.

She nodded at me but her face was red.

I gave her a hug and then another one. I wanted her to be okay before we had to go back to our groups. I stayed until her counselor had gotten her to calm down and then walked back to my own cabin in a daze, trying to sort out what I'd learned and whether I should be as concerned as the man with the beard believed I should be. I was miffed at him for stirring things up and upsetting Nava and me. We had been fine until he showed up.

I decided to shrug off the encounter. I didn't want anybody to worry about me.

After talking with us, the man got our home number from the camp director and called my father to let him know that what my mother was involved with was dangerous and that he should be concerned. My father said he already knew that; he had been following Bhagwan and the ranch in the news and cutting out articles from the paper for months.

When I was grown my father told me he had never discussed the cult with Nava and me because he didn't want to frighten us about the danger he thought my mother faced. The ranch in Antelope had more arms, he said, than the local Oregon police, including a large arsenal of Uzis. There was one road leading into the commune, Ma Anand Sheela was a fanatic, and my father worried it was another Jonestown waiting to happen.

~

Two weeks after the cult educator visited, Nava and I each got a Susan Seddon-Boulet card from my mother in the camp mail; mine was of a goddess. We knew the artwork well—ethereal and mythical, spiritual and ghostly, we'd seen Seddon-Boulet's paintings in my mother's apartment. They were images of shamans and animal-people against dark swirls of color with transparent orbs floating in the space around them. The goddess on my card—the face of patient wisdom—made the message from my mother more potent.

Inside she wrote that she was having a good time at Rancho Rajneesh and she wouldn't be coming home when she'd originally said she would. That she would stay the rest of the summer.

I got permission and walked to Nava's cabin, my throat aching like part of it had been torn. I followed the path from the teen side of camp to the junior side watching myself as if from above, my mother's news slicing through and separating me from my body.

I went to where Nava huddled with her counselor, my sister's thin arms and legs tanned from almost five weeks in the outdoors. Someone must have done her hair because the front of each side was neatly pulled into a small elastic, the rest of it was down. She was so little at ten years old and when we made eye contact, we both started crying.

I tried to talk but I couldn't breathe right. My words were halting, interrupted with each jerk of my chest. My mother's message had cracked me open, split the shell I had built around myself all these years. What I had taken in stride up until now—the unease I had about her going to the ranch in the first place, when she'd so recently been looking at apartments for the three of us, poured out of me.

Now Nava and I were both sobbing. I wanted to stop so I could take care of her but fresh tears streamed down my face. "It's okay," I managed to stutter out, sniffling and trying catch my breath.

Were my mother and me only connected because I wanted to be? What would happen if I stopped reaching out offering pieces of myself to her? Would we have a relationship at all?

~

I grew quieter after I returned from camp. Eighth grade had begun, I'd just turned thirteen, and I doubted my mother was going to make it back for my fall bat mitzvah, the Jewish coming of age ritual for girls. Not only did I miss her, the relationship I once had with my father, the one where he confided in me and I confided in him, where we were each other's biggest fans, was over.

His bursts of anger continued, and when we were in the apartment together I tried to keep my distance. Home was my least favorite place to be. I not only fully rejected the job of homemaker and partner to my father that for years I had actively pursued, I didn't want to see him at all. I was becoming a young woman with no other woman to protect me from slipping into the role I now rejected. I couldn't pretend I was comfortable around him. I couldn't pretend we were close anymore.

I asked Nava to take over making and bringing coffee to him in the mornings. At bedtime now when he tucked me in, I turned my head so it wouldn't be easy for him to kiss me goodnight. I started putting heavy face cream or sometimes a thin coating of Vaseline on my cheeks. "You don't want to get this on you," I'd say, looking up at him with my head pushed into my pillow as far from him as was possible, almost challenging him to try. Each night was a new chance to avoid his affection. It never occurred to me until I had children of my own that their need for more space as they become teenagers, more physical autonomy, is absolutely normal; that parents should expect that distance. I didn't know I could tell him that. I never said, "I don't want kisses at night anymore." In part I was afraid of hurting his feelings or making him mad, and I also worried how he would take my rejection; whether he would reject me in return, which wasn't something I could risk.

I saw my best friend Claudia or kept to myself most of the time, and I regret I left Nava alone. I'm sure she wondered why I didn't want to talk much or spend time with her.

The only time the apartment felt good was when my father was at work.

Apart from Celeste, I had been critical of my father's girlfriends, hoping they'd hit the road. Now I had the role I had longed for back when we lived with Tracy, Sara, and Janine in Ivy Hill—it appeared I had won my father, the prize. But being his confidant was the last thing I wanted. I found myself wishing for a woman—even Tracy—to come into his life so he could remarry. I needed someone to save me from being the woman of the house. But the ladies were gone, and my mother was far away.

My mood darkened. I had bought diet pills from a corner pharmacy to help me at least feel better on the outside, but they didn't seem to be working. I was still bigger than I wanted to be and I started wearing black every day. I must have mentioned to Claudia that I wasn't happy, or made an offhand comment, because she spoke with my father in private, making him promise not to tell me where he'd heard I was thinking of suicide. He booked our family an appointment with a therapist and forbade me to wear anymore black clothes. So, doing what any teenager would do, I stuffed my black miniskirts and black sweaters into my backpack, snuck them out of the house, and put them on as soon as I left the apartment in the mornings.

The day of our therapy appointment came, and the three of us made our way down the crowded streets of Flushing in the dimming light of late afternoon. We headed north on Main Street and under the bridge. We passed the stands with cheap earrings and jelly shoes and trinkets for sale. We walked past Barone's pizza, toward the crowds oozing up from the 7 subway station below, but on this day I couldn't examine the myriad faces around me, analyzing expressions like I usually did. I was too nervous. I didn't know what to expect having never been to counseling before and was fearful about what the therapist would uncover; scared she would see the truth and let my secret out. I didn't want my father or anyone to know I was growing uneasy around him. My mission was to make sure I revealed nothing.

We sat in the therapist's office, the three of us on a small fabric sofa. Her name was Patty and she sat in her chair facing us. All three of her lamps threw soft yellow light into the room. She had grey eyes with brown wavy hair and bangs. I stared at my lap, stealing glances at Patty. Nava sat next to me. As usual, I had put Nava between my father and me—my human shield. Her hair was slightly disheveled with flyaway bangs and an elastic hair tie at the back of her head sprouting a curling, unbrushed ponytail.

There I was, my hands clasped tightly together in my lap. Fortifying myself, smiling when it was called for. I made sure to pepper the conversation with some of my time-tested repartee, the watchman inside me alert, the flashlight beaming out at my new surroundings, trying to read the room so I could land on my feet and spring if necessary. I knew I had to hide how I was feeling, fold it over itself and smash it. Stomp the unsettled and confused part of myself down so nobody knew about it.

We talked for a while and then Patty handed the three of us a blank sheet of paper and some crayons and asked us to draw a picture of our family. I knew that she was trying to figure something out and I needed to be careful with my picture. I didn't want her to think I enjoyed spending time with my father so, just like I no longer washed my clothing with his when I did the laundry on Friday nights in the basement laundry room of our apartment, just like I no longer sat next to him when I could avoid it, I drew a picture for Patty where my figure was far left in the frame. I drew Nava, my buffer, close to me, and after that, next to her, my father. I knew I was on the right track but just for good measure I decided to draw our blue pet parakeet Joey huge above our heads, because, I rationalized, he, in his cage and removed from our family was better off than any of the three of us. I figured it couldn't hurt to confuse Patty a little more. By adding our pet, I aimed to make my inner life more mysterious; I wanted to show I was not an easy nut to crack.

We all finished our pictures and Patty took them. She didn't say anything for a while, only studied them. My father had drawn a basic family-of-three picture; no intrigue, no drama, nothing notable in it. Nava had drawn a picture of my father kicking a hole in my bedroom door. She asked Nava and my father to go to the waiting room.

When we were alone which I was relieved about but still scared, she said, "Does your dad sometimes feel too much like a friend?"

"What do you mean?" I blurted out too fast.

She explained that I seemed to have drawn myself as far from him as I could.

I felt so stupid for doing my picture that way. I couldn't believe I had been found out. Part of me wanted to know this was a genuine problem, a normal concern about too much closeness and that I was not alone in feeling unsettled. Another part of me did not want to name my discomfort for fear of it becoming more real. I did my best to answer with as little affect as I could and get out of there quickly.

Nava talked with Patty, privately, too, and when I was sitting in the waiting room with my father, I didn't speak to him. I could hardly look at him. I was mortified. How could this secret hidden part in me have become so obvious? How could this worry that had been churning inside me now be turning into such a solid shape it was observable by a stranger? Maybe, I thought, it was me. Maybe I was wrong about our relationship, what I had felt, what I had experienced. Maybe I was the only one with the problem.

It was my father's turn next and he went in. Waiting for him with Nava next to me, I remembered sitting next to him on the couch at home about a month before, practicing the Hebrew for my bat mitzvah. He'd asked me to grab my notebook and meet him in the living room so he could coach me. We sat on the couch next to each other and I tucked myself into the right most corner near the armrest in an effort to give myself some space from him. He sat close on the other side of me. He stretched his right arm behind me and rested it on the back cushions. Without getting up I shifted my body away from him further into the side I was hugging. I didn't know why he sat so near me. I didn't know why we couldn't practice the portion at the dining room table.

I wish I'd had the confidence to tell him to give me more space— or that I'd had the nerve to get up and move. It seems like such a small thing to me now, but I didn't have the belief that what I wanted was as important as what he wanted. And, I felt if I had to ask for it, it wouldn't have given me what I really wanted and had wanted for so long—for him to just recognize what I needed and act on it. For he and my mother to treat me like a child, whose needs have to be intuited. I was so tired of waiting for them to recognize that.

I read my *Torah* portion from my spot on the couch but began to feel his breath on me. We were close enough that it tickled my neck. I tried to ignore the sensation, but it gave me a shivery feeling. I continued to read, but it was hard for me to focus. With each of his exhalations, I fought off a shiver.

Now, waiting outside Patty's office for my father to come out, I wondered why I'd stayed there so close to him. What did that say about me?

I sat quietly in the waiting room with Nava, my horror growing. If this was not something only I was aware of, if it wasn't just me, and my father felt the undercurrent in our relationship too, what would happen? How could I face him? What was I supposed to do if we were honest about our situation? I had nowhere else to live. Nowhere else to go emotionally.

When we left Patty's office it was dark outside. I felt as if my insides had been pulled out like stuffing from a damaged plush toy. We walked south on Main Street, me trailing these just-unearthed parts of myself. Who was going to take care of them? I was better off before I'd dug them up.

We hadn't had dinner yet. We passed the Burger King and I wished we could eat there, but we never had fast food with my father. My mother was the one who used to get us that kind of food on weekends. Tonight we were going to go home and we were going to open two Hungry Man cans of soup. One for my father, one for Nava and me to split. None of us talked on the way to our apartment. We didn't know what to say.

~

For my bat mitzvah that October, my father invited his boss and a lot of the staff, including the secretaries whose pencils Nava and I had sharpened over the years during our visits to the office. Grandma Doris from California flew to New York for the first time in decades, and my Aunt Ellen and her family arrived. Aunt Ellen had taken me to shop for my dress. I wore heavy eye makeup to school and short skirts with tights or even fishnet stockings like I saw in music videos, so there had been some concern I might not understand how to pick out a dress appropriate for the occasion. Aunt Ellen met me at Macy's in Manhattan and steered me in the direction of a tasteful and fashion-forward dress-and-blazer combination in champagne-colored rayon and satin.

All of my mother's family from Brooklyn attended: My Uncle Bobby and his kids, Aunt Gloria, and my cigar-smoking Grandpa Frank. Everyone came, except my mother.

On the morning of my bat mitzvah, thunder boomed and a leak sprung in the roof of the synagogue. When I was up at the bimah reciting my Torah portion, the often-irritable rabbi whispered to me, "Slow down," so the guests in the sanctuary could have at least a shot at understanding what I was saying. I, in my smart-ass way, not missing a beat, slowed my Hebrew way, way down to a crawl. "B-a-r-u-c-h-a-t-t-a," I continued, leaving whole seconds between syllables to exaggerate the rabbi's direction and to cover up my embarrassment at his publicly correcting me. I was pleased when I heard a warm ripple of laughter in the sanctuary. My sass had paid off. I had cleverly proven to anyone in attendance that this event my mother hadn't shown up for wasn't that important to me. I finished my speech, and after the refreshments we had a small gathering with my extended family at our favorite Italian restaurant, Bacigalup's.

At the post-bat mitzvah refreshment hour, we gathered in the small, wood-paneled reception room for cake and mazel tovs.

"There she is!" Aunt Gloria called in her Sheepshead Bay accent when I entered.

"Look at you!" she said, holding my hands out and grinning. She glanced at my uncle and cousins who stood next to her. "Look at her! You did such a good job, my darling. *So* articulate. *So* gorgeous!"

"You could really read all that? With no help?" Uncle Bobby asked, shoving a raspberry rugelach in his mouth.

"Oh, I had to practice for a while," I answered, and hugged his daughters, who leaned into me.

I could see they were happy for me, and I was grateful all my relatives had come out—I was the first grandchild on both sides, the first niece.

I went over to where Grandpa Frank sat in a metal folding chair. "Thank you for being here, Grandpa."

He hadn't been the best parent to his kids but when he took me for that first slice of pizza in Brooklyn all those years ago, I had felt safe. He squeezed my hand from where he sat as if to say, *I'm here even if she isn't*, his eyes twinkling through a half-glaze. "Mazel tov," he said, "Ronit, you did a good job."

I smelled the sweet burnt trace of his last cigar on him. His pale blue eyes seemed to take in more than he let on. I knew he disapproved of my mother's choices. I had heard him say to her before, "How could you leave those beautiful girls?" I had seen her walk away from him when he asked.

I told myself it wasn't so bad that my mother wasn't there. The bat mitzvah itself wasn't especially important to me. I was Jewish, I had been born in Israel, I went to Hebrew school so of course I would have one, but I didn't see it as more than a right of passage and something I was expected to do. Though I did understand how poorly it reflected on my mother that she wasn't there. If I was sad, I kept the sadness hidden even from myself. I watered down the experience so I could swallow it without doing harm to myself. But I would in future years pull out the fact of her absence to highlight neglect, or when I needed someone to understand in a nutshell how I grew up. One of my abandoned-by-my-mother one-liners.

When my father, Nava, and I said goodbye to everyone and got home, I took off my high heels and opened my gift envelopes in the living room, checks fluttering to the floor. I gave them to my father to deposit, gathered my cards into a stack, and brought them to my bedroom. It was late afternoon and the sun was already setting below the apartment building across our alley. I had hit my marks that day but, like a stage actor at the end of a long run, I couldn't muster much feeling about it.

I sat on my bed in the dress my aunt had helped me buy. I'd put my hair up by myself as best as I could that morning in my version of a French twist, but most of it had escaped by the time we'd all gone to lunch; more tendrils were now down around my face than up. I pulled out my hair clip and bobby pins and dropped them on my night table. I was never good at doing my hair, not like my mother was.

Sometimes even though I was thirteen I'd see someone walking in Flushing who for a moment I thought looked like my mother. I wanted so much for it to be her; I'd peer at the dark-haired woman from across the street or half a block away until I was certain it wasn't. Other times I'd let myself imagine that she'd come to surprise me and it would take my breath away. I'd be heading down to Main Street to get a slice at Barone's and I'd pretend I saw her emerge from the tide of people approaching me. Or I would be picking out a new belt under the bridge and let myself feel what it would be like to turn and see she was right there standing next to me. My mother, the elusive. My mother, the gift.

But now the day was over. My room was getting dark. She was all I wanted but she was not there.

Alone in a Group

It was Halloween night three weeks after my bat mitzvah. I was dressed as a cave girl, and I had lost my friends in the dark. I was wearing a flesh-colored bodysuit underneath a cavewoman tunic made of fake fur and the inside of the acrylic fabric was rough. I ran my finger along the edge to pull it away from my neck where it kept rubbing against my skin. I had a dog's toy bone in my hair and a faded blue pillowcase for a trick-or-treat bag. I had helped organize our group of six to meet that night at 6:30 and travel together up and down the apartment buildings along Kissena Boulevard.

This was the first Halloween my father had allowed me to go out in the neighborhood with only my friends. Up to that point Nava and I had trick-or-treated together in our apartment building, first in Ivy Hill and then in Flushing. But this year I had petitioned my father to walk the neighborhood without an adult nearby, and he had said yes. For the first time I was spending Halloween like a teenager.

Now, I stood on the corner, the skin on my bare legs and arms prickling in the light wind that had picked up, trying to figure out which direction my friends, Claudia and four boys we knew from Junior High School 189, had gone. Groups of adults and costumed children moved by me in clusters, entering and exiting the apartment buildings that lined the street in all directions.

My friends and I had walked a block together when an unsupervised pack of kids in regular clothes chased after us, scattering us in all directions, yelling, "That's right, you better run," and, "We're going to get you!" The pack of kids was gone now and so were my friends.

I could turn back home, toward my apartment building two blocks away, or I could head south. I usually didn't go that direction unless I was walking to the "Y" with Claudia, which was where she and I had been swimming together since fourth grade. I knew I'd pass the candy store where we bought and wolfed down chips and chocolate bars after hours in the pool. I'd pass the apartment building where Grandpa Sammy had lived before he moved to Florida, and the fruit stand where last summer the wife of the owner had told me to stop cherry-picking from the flat of Bings. Since I knew the area, I decided to search for my friends. I hadn't made the point about being old enough and mature enough when I begged my father to let me go out tonight only to return home thirty minutes after leaving the apartment. All I had to do was find Claudia and the boys and pick up where we'd left off. I began my walk south.

I'd gone a block when I saw a group of kids headed in my direction. Relieved, I began walking faster toward them.

Trying to make out their faces in the dark, I called, "Hey guys!"

As I got closer, I saw they seemed shorter than my friends. And there were too many of them. I had almost reached them when I realized they were the pack of girls and boys that had chased us. My stomach clenched.

If I hadn't drawn attention to myself I might have been able to hide or maybe walk past them. But they had heard me. They stopped right in front of me, blocking by path.

There were seven of them and they ranged in age from nine years old to thirteen. The biggest boy was my height. I didn't entertain the idea of running away; I wasn't fast. But I also wasn't tough; I'd never hit anybody except for Nava.

I decided that if I showed them I was nice and meant them no trouble they'd leave me alone. I needed to pretend that I wasn't out of my element; I needed to pretend I wasn't afraid.

I opened my eyes wide, hoping they would see I was harmless, and in my friendliest voice I said, "Excuse me, have you by any chance seen a group of kids trick-or-treating?"

They stared back at me with flat expressions.

"A group of kids trick-or-treating?" the oldest kid asked. He seemed like the leader.

"Yes," I said. It was a good sign the leader was talking me. I described a few of their costumes and kept my face open, hopeful.

"Yeah," he said, looking back toward his posse and I noticed a kind of amusement on his friends' faces. "I think we did." He gestured in the direction I was headed. "That way."

"Over there? Great! Thank you so much."

"Oh, sure," he said. His eyes were engaged, but his face was inscrutable.

"I'm going to go find them," I said cheerily. "Thanks again!"

I took a step to the left to go around them but he blocked me with his arm. I laughed lightly as if I had misunderstood and took a step to the right. This time he draped his arm around my shoulder and pulled me next to him.

"You know what," he said, "let's go find them together."

With his arm on my shoulder he steered me south and we started walking. His friends followed closely behind. I played it cool and kept moving with him, as if this was the most natural thing in the world to be going somewhere with this guy I didn't know, this guy whose arm was squeezing me tight; holding me in place.

I scanned the streets for my friends as he took us south another block; I searched for a safe place to run from them but there was nowhere to go. When we got to the curb in front of the fruit stand, I reached my hands up to take his arm off me but it was too late. He wrapped it around my neck and tightened his grip.

"Wait, wait," I said through the boy's chokehold. I was speaking to him, to the gang of them, but he pressed his arm harder against my neck.

A switch had been flipped and we stopped pretending now.

The kids crowded around me and shouted, taking their turns to push me. I was in the middle of their circle, their noise. The leader forced me down and my knees were on cement.

I kept talking like it could save me, as if all I had to do is make what I needed from them clearer and they would realize they'd made a mistake, that this was a misunderstanding. Like if I could figure out what I had done wrong they would stop.

I felt something hit me in the back. Then in the shoulder. Something else swooshed past my ear. I ducked, my arms over my head, my eyes focused on the grain in the dark gray sidewalk. An apple rolled into my line of vision. A pear. That's when I understood. Fruit. They were taking fruit off the fruit stand and throwing it at me. I couldn't even get beat up in a normal way.

I tried to look up in between each round of their assault to scan the space beyond their heads. How could this happen? People were out tonight. Nobody was coming to help. An adult had to stop.

Standing just inside where his awning began I saw the grocer at the fruit stand, his face ghostly in the fluorescence of his overhead lighting. For a moment I was able to meet his eyes. He could be the one to tell the kids to leave me alone. He could chase them away from his stand. He could even call the police. But he stayed where he was, watching.

When I saw a grapefruit coming, I turned to cover my face but it smacked me in the jaw. It rolled to the ground. I saw it flash rubbery yellow against the rough pavement. I curled down around myself to protect my body.

A minute passed and the kids' laughter subsided. Then the fruit stopped. Then their voices sounded farther away. I waited until I was sure they had left before I moved. I didn't know why they had quit; I didn't understand why they had started. In the gutter in front of me were clumped old leaves, a few Now and Later wrappers, cigarette butts, and a crushed McDonald's coffee cup.

Clutching my pillowcase, I wobbled up to standing.

My knees were scraped. My ponytail had fallen out; I'd lost my bone. I glanced north and I glanced south. Cars drove past me on Kissena Blvd and, stepping out of the road and onto the curb, I began the walk home. The windows in the apartment buildings I passed glowed against the darkness outside.

I was alert like I had been on the walk home with Janine and Tracy after the mugging on that snowy night in New Jersey and with my mother the night of her Est party near Central Park when the man followed us. I moved quickly and with all of my senses alive, almost holding my breath until I got to the lobby of my apartment building.

The doorman stopped me before I opened the glass doors. I couldn't come in, he said. I live here, I told him. No, he said. He didn't know me and thought I was a teenager up to mischief. "Please," I pleaded, trying to catch my breath. "Buzz my father, apartment 333. He'll tell you." The doorman didn't look convinced but rang my father, and soon Nava came down and told the doorman he had to let me in, pounding on his chest when he wouldn't budge.

When we got up to our apartment and I told both of them what had happened, I saw Nava's face crumple into worry for me, into sadness. My father listened but didn't say anything. His eyes were unreadable. The only sign that he was upset was how his jaw clenched. I wouldn't ask my father to go trick-or-treating again and we wouldn't talk about this after tonight.

When I got to the bathroom mirror, I saw my costume was torn, my eye makeup was running, and I had shaving cream on my back which I hadn't felt the kids spray on me. I cleaned myself up, and still shivering from being out in the cold, crawled into my bed.

I was thankful Nava was already asleep—that she wouldn't ever have to know how my chest shook in the dark or see the tears I could no longer control.

The Missing Piece

The last time I saw my mother in New York was shortly after the Halloween I got shaving-creamed and pummeled by fruit. It was early November 1985 and she had just returned from six months at the ranch in Oregon, where things had fallen apart.

Tensions between Rancho Rajneesh and Antelope residents had been escalating. In an effort to prevent voters from threatening the future of Rancho Rajneesh, Bhagwan's top aides had successfully infected salad bars in local restaurants with salmonella they had cultivated in their very own Rajneeshee labs, sickening more than seven hundred people and sending forty-five to local hospitals. This was the largest bioterror attack on U.S. soil.

An affidavit presented by Oregon State Police Lieutenant Dean Renfrow to the Jefferson County District Court on October 1, 1985, as described in *The Rajneesh Chronicles*, contains a description of an apparent biological-warfare laboratory at Rajneeshpuram. There was enough evidence in the affidavit "implicating members of the Rajneesh Medical Corporation and other individual Rajneeshees in the most frightening of crimes and criminal plots, including the waging of biological warfare against the people of The Dalles," (the largest community in Oregon's Wasco County), "through the spreading of salmonella in the town's restaurants and an attempted poisoning of its water supply, the poisoning of Jefferson County District Attorney Mike Sullivan and Wasco County Court Commissioner William Hulse and attempted poisonings of Rajneesh disciples who were out of favor with top commune officials…as well as the drugging of a number of Rajneesh disciples."

On October 27, 1985, Bhagwan, always one to look out for himself, fled his ranch. Sannyasins watched his private plane suddenly take off, carrying him, his personal physician, and a small entourage. They were headed for Bermuda to avoid Bhagwan's arrest but his plane was intercepted at a fuel stop in Charlotte, North Carolina. Bhagwan was served with a 35-count indictment charging him and seven of his followers with conspiracy and fraud in immigration matters. He was deported to India on November 17, 1985.

Soon after, the ranch began shutting down. Greyhound buses pulled in, loaded up sannyasins, and pulled out. Thousands of people were faced with leaving the home they thought would be theirs forever. Rancho Rajneesh was over. The businesses they had created, the infrastructure they had built, the crops they had planted; the community they had nurtured were no more.

My mother and the other sannyasins had given up all their possessions for their guru, and were now leaderless and without a plan. She had left everything she owned in New York in Karma's care but Karma was nowhere to be found. She had moved into my mother's apartment while she was away and then let the lease lapse. When my mother tracked Karma's mother down and called her to ask where her daughter had gone, her mother said, "I'm not helping her out this time." Apparently, she was a serial swindler.

Karma had maxed out my mother's credit cards and except for the few pieces my father had managed to pick up from Karma one day earlier that fall, all of her furniture was gone. My father later told me that while he packed up the old Persian rug my mother had inherited from her mother, a framed print, a round ivory end table, and the blue velvet sofa, Karma had come onto him.

Though my mother no longer had an apartment to return to, when she fled the ranch she came back to New York. My father had a business trip planned so he told her she could stay with us at our apartment and watch us while she figured things out.

In a photo of Nava, my mother, and me from that time, my mother looks unusually thin. Hollows carve shadows under her cheeks, and her complexion is off; her face has a pale, yellow hue. She has a faint smile but it doesn't reach her eyes. Nava, ten and a half, dangles from her left arm, and I, a little chubby and, as usual, wearing too much makeup, have my arm around my mother's shoulder. I lean into her, a big stretched-out smile across my face, as if she is dazzling to me, despite the fact that she'd already left us twice. I think my attachment confounded my father, too. He was the one who had taken care of Nava and me most of our childhood.

Even though I should have known better, I still imagined my mother appearing fairy queen-like and changing my life. She was the missing piece, the part that, when returned to me, would allow me to live my true life. She was the one who could give my world shape.

But sitting there with her in our living room on the couch—finally just the three of us again—I didn't know how to act. She wasn't making conversation and I didn't know what to say to her. I turned to my default behavior and tried to be useful.

"Do you want some tea?" I asked.

"No, thanks," she said.

"Are you chilly? Do you want a blanket?" I asked, bringing one over. Thankfully, she took it, otherwise I would have been positive I was annoying her. Nava cuddled up to her but I didn't want to sit too close; my mother seemed like she needed space. She held herself somewhat apart from us, her arms crossed and folded close to her chest, her expressions dull, her movements measured. It wasn't the reunion I had hoped for or imagined.

Dusky November light filtered in through our windows, the city's mandatory child safety bars partially obstructing the view of the other brick buildings across the alley, the mostly bare branches of several trees clawing up to the darkening sky.

I don't know if she was unhappy with being back or just distracted, but she didn't seem excited to be with us. Instead of her working hard to win my love or make things better, there I was again, hoping I wouldn't chase her off. Hoping she liked me. The only difference from the early years with her was that I knew unequivocally I couldn't have done anything to make her angry; I hadn't seen her in six months.

I worried if I said the wrong thing, or touched her without warning, or got too close, she'd disappear again. I watched her face, made a joke, tried to be pleasing, whatever I figured that was.

I didn't realize how shallowly I was breathing or recognize my restraint. I had none of the casual comfort I might have had with her if she'd never left. I watched her when she talked, went into overdrive trying to read her for signs of distress. I analyzed the features of her face to collect them into an image I could understand, to interpret what she meant. I read her disorientation upon returning to New York as reserve and standoffishness. It drove me to search for what I could do to bring her nearer to me. This was, after all, a beginning. She was back and we could start again. I was ready.

I couldn't appreciate it then, but she probably was on edge and uncertain about being with us in her ex-husband's apartment. Maybe she should have known better than to accept, and maybe my father should have known better than to offer. His agitation was apparent soon after he came home from work that afternoon before he left for his trip.

"Hi!" I called to him while he put his briefcase down.

"Hi," he answered with a flat voice. He nodded to my mother. I wanted him to be friendly to her, but he didn't come into the living room; instead, he went into his bedroom to change.

After about twenty minutes he came out and I got him to take a few photos of the three of us, and then Nava and I sat trying to visit with my mother, but I was distracted. My father's footsteps were heavy. He stomped to the kitchen for water. Stomped back to his room. Now he was in the hallway banging cabinets. We heard him approaching, muttering to himself.

He stood in the dining room facing us and cursed at her, calling her a terrible name.

"Give me the child support you owe!" he yelled out of nowhere. He scanned the dining room table for something and cursed again.

Like a bird being flushed from a bush my mother got up and tried to move past him and I got up to follow her. Nava followed me. I didn't know where we were going, but I couldn't sit and watch her fend him off alone.

"Give me the money!" He snatched her purse off the table. "Is it here?" he shouted, waving her purse and digging through it. "Here?"

My eyes darted from him to my mother, who looked scared, the panic in me growing as I tried to figure out what I could do to make this better, how I could make him stop.

She grabbed her suitcase and went to the hallway to get away from him, ready to leave her purse. He caught the apartment door as it closed and swung it back open. He followed her out yelling, calling her names.

He threw her purse onto the stained burgundy carpet. "Where is the money? Where is the money?" he yelled, his eyes blazing, his face burning with anger.

My mother swooped down to get her purse but tripped and ended up on the ground.

I was ready to spring into movement, ready to make them stop fighting, but was frozen in place. How could I help? Stand in front of my mother? Grab the purse and run? I didn't know which to do. I didn't know what to say. I stood in the doorway, my hands suspended in front of me, palms out.

My father grabbed the purse strap and tugged at it.

"Dad, stop," I said.

That's when our elderly neighbor, Elizabeth from England, whose apartment next to the garbage room was just beyond where my mother now crouched, opened her door to investigate the racket. From my place at our threshold I saw our family the way she must have.

There my mother knelt on old, matted carpet, clutching her purse while my father pulled at its handle, her thin scarf dragging on the stained hallway carpet, the warm garbage stink of the incinerator room filling the airless hallway.

I looked up at Elizabeth. She looked at me.

Seeing her witnessing us in that moment made me realize we weren't going to recover from this. *I* couldn't recover from it. It didn't matter how much I wished we could be okay. Elizabeth seeing us made it worse, made me realize we were never going to be a good family.

Nava was having trouble breathing. I left the hallway and took her inside to the living room window and opened it for fresh air.

My father let go of the purse, my mother said goodbye and left. The next we heard from her, she said she was moving across the country, to Seattle. Without us.

~

That week, I sat by myself in the schoolyard before classes started, out of words for friends. Out of words for myself. One more layer of me had been peeled off. Gone was the part that had been able to pretend I was doing all right with things the way they were.

I had survived living the way we did because in my heart I believed that soon life would be different; soon my mother, Nava, and I would be together again in some way. But I finally knew the truth. My mother was never coming back.

On My Way

A year later my father would begin dating Judy, the woman who would become my stepmom, and I would start ninth grade at Bayside High School, where I didn't know anyone among the roughly 2,000 students. I spent most of my lunch times hiding in a corner of the school library reading up about the Donner Party tragedy, animal rights, and vegetarianism while I snuck bites of smuggled-in cheese sandwiches every day for most of the school year.

I met a Bayside boy from a large Irish Catholic family who sat behind me in English and teased me about how much I loved cats, but ultimately became dear to me. Kieran had my back, especially when word got to him via his swim team friends that the boys in my swim class were sniggering at my see-through bathing suit. It wasn't supposed to be see-through but I'd had it since sixth grade, and it was stretched out and threadbare since I hadn't thought to ask for a new one. That embarrassing conversation with Kieran cemented our bond. We wrote letters to each other in the summers and I pined for a family as big and seemingly stable as his.

I came back to Bayside that fall for tenth grade with a perm and better clothes. Judy, a former actress turned therapist with a love of jewelry, perfume, and talking about feelings, made it a point to take Nava and me back-to-school-shopping. I had never been so grateful as I was for this woman. She helped free me up to go through adolescence the way other girls got to, and cooked beautiful meals for us all so I didn't have to.

I had lots of friends in tenth grade, sang solos in chorus, joined student government, and took honors Latin, History, French, and English. I had big hair and went to toga parties for Latin club, had crushes on boys, and wore lots of eyeshadow. One night on the phone Kieran told me, in the same gentle way he had when I inadvertently flashed my swim class the year before, that *maybe* I might want to consider toning down the eye makeup. It seemed my very made-up face was a topic of discussion in our class. I was a little hurt but mostly grateful to him for letting me know.

I had plans with friends almost every weekend and got to dress up and go to sweet sixteen parties. I was growing taller and slimming out—I could even make out some cheekbones. Finally, I felt, I was becoming the girl I had wanted to be.

Unfortunately, I left Bayside the next fall after my father and Judy married. We moved away from Flushing to Port Washington on the North Shore of Long Island where I started a new high school as a junior. This school, my sixth in ten years, would be my final one before college. For the first six months I spent there, I would ask my father and Judy to please let me return to my old high school. I begged them to let me take the Long Island Railroad to and from Bayside every school day. Eventually, though, I made friends at my new school and got good roles in plays. My old classmates used lots of black eyeliner and Aqua-Net, my new classmates wore Docksiders and listened to classic rock. Some even owned boats.

People had lawns and backyards, there were almost no buildings higher than three stories, and old trees lined the roads. After years of bars-on-windows apartment living, waiting for and wondering when my real life would begin, or at least be one I liked, I had ended up in this pastoral place. I was going to go to college and leave my growing up years behind. It looked like I was on my way, or at least I had a good shot of making it out in one piece.

Memorial Day night of senior year I lay on the sand at Bar Beach with my friends. I had seen fireworks on TV and in movies but never in person. My friends giggled and goofed around nearby and I breathed in the humid Long Island night, the air already too warm for May.

My father was home with Judy, Nava at a sleepover. I wondered what my mother was doing that night in Seattle. Did she miss me? Did she think about me during her day the way I did about her? Although we spoke once or twice a week and Nava and I had gone to visit her during the past few summers, I had no real sense of her life there.

It took me many years and a lot of therapy—plus becoming a mother myself—but I came to understand that my mother didn't leave because of me. She left because of who she was, what she didn't have, and what she thought she needed.

In order to survive I needed to believe I had the power to change her mind, that I could find a way to make her stay. I didn't realize for a long time, not until I had children myself, that it wasn't up to me to keep her with me. I couldn't have faced that truth when I was young because then, besides not having her with me, I no longer would have had hope that I could ever get her back.

My relationship with her would change over the years, especially once I was married and had my daughter and my son. When they were babies and toddlers and then school age, I'd sometimes catch myself wondering how my mother could have walked out on Nava and me when we were that young. Even imagining leaving them could crush the air out of me. For me, being their mother, having this family, has satisfied a profound space within me and has also shown me how much I missed growing up.

Recognizing again and again how different my mothering is from how she mothered has been a cure for, and also the source of my pain.

But before I knew I would get married and have two children, before I knew we would live in Seattle, and that she and I would grow to have what might resemble a regular mother-daughter relationship, I had a glimpse that I might be okay after all.

That night on the beach, Memorial Day of senior year, I let my body rest in the cool sand. Looking up, I watched firework after firework burst into the black sky and rain down, held by their shimmering spell. For several moments they seemed to be reaching out only toward me, showing me how beautiful, how exciting, how unknown my life still could be, how big the world was—and I wasn't scared.

Epilogue

In December, 2019 I sat with my mother after a Shabbat dinner she'd prepared for our family, which she does almost every week. We live five minutes from each other now, and my father, who splits time between Seattle and Manhattan, is often at the table too. We gather at sundown on these Fridays—me, my husband, my daughter, my son, my mother, and my father. We say the blessings over the candles, the wine, and the challah, and my father gives what he calls "Grandpa's blessing."

My mother is an astounding cook—as good as, if not better than, in her kibbutz kitchen days. Stews, briskets, steaks for those who eat those things and ziti, lasagna, Indian daal, falafel, and soups for vegetarians like me and my father. I wish I cooked like her but am very happy to have my mother do it. It's a relief to have her prepare meals for me once again.

When my children were small my stepmom, Judy—now divorced from my father—came to visit us in Seattle, and she thought it was interesting that I had, as she described it, recreated my family of childhood here in Seattle so many years later. I'm not precisely sure what her intention was in sharing that with me, but at the time I was self-conscious and wondered if what I was doing was strange; that inviting my parents who had been divorced for forty years—four times as long as they'd been married—over for dinner every week was delusional in some way. I think now I understand that my ex-stepmom might have had feelings about this. After all, she took over when I was in high school, years when my mother was absent from my life except for summer visits to Seattle. She was the one who had made my teenage years more bearable, who handled the cooking and let me shop for new clothes before school began in the fall, who offered a buffer between me and my father. And yet I was closer to my mother now.

I see in a way how it could seem odd, or worse in my view, infantile, to settle my young family in the city where my family of origin collapsed. That I was playing at some make believe game, pretending that nothing was ever wrong or painful about our history together. But I can also appreciate that I've learned to take what I can get. Not the way I did as a kid when I had no choice, but on my terms.

Maybe that's a form of settling, but it feels right to have my parents here with me. And it's funny when they joke around together. At Shabbat dinner recently my father announced that he and my mother would have been celebrating their fiftieth wedding anniversary had they not gotten divorced. My mother kind of nodded and shrugged her shoulders, as if to say, *all right already, we know, we know.* They've gotten closer over the years and Nava and I have wondered if they ever feel getting divorced wasn't worth it in the end. They still see each other frequently, share time with their kids and grandkids and even meet for coffee sometimes, just the two of them. They might have saved us a lot of trouble if they'd tried to make it work.

When I was in my early twenties and first trying to understand why relationships were hard for me, a therapist said to me that I must be angry at my mother, that really there couldn't be a way I wasn't. I sat there, searching my body for signs of this anger, for any feeling in my chest that this was true for me but I couldn't find it. I knew it should be there but I didn't feel it.

But later, I did. When I had my own children, it would rise up sometimes when I saw my mother tucking my daughter in, cuddling my son, cooking up brunch for my family. I was angry that my kids got to experience her as a maternal figure when I had not, angry that she never addressed how strange it was, her being around for *their* childhood and not mine—angry my kids got her and I didn't. I realized later that I could never have had that anger as a teenager or young adult because I couldn't afford it. Back then I couldn't risk driving her away.

Because I get to see my mother regularly now, I dissect her the way lots of teenage girls dissect their mothers, with the luxury of time and familiarity and most importantly; without having to worry she'll leave.

One night after I thought I'd just finished writing this book, we sat on the sofa together. My husband had to take a call and my kids had agreed to a game of Monopoly in the other room with my father. I don't know how the conversation about our past started but I knew pretty quickly we were heading to a place we hadn't been in a long time, or maybe had never been, at least quite in this way. From the other room I could hear dogs squeaking their toys, my husband on his call, and my father laughing at something the kids did.

But in the living room where I sat facing my mother on the sofa, I shut all of them out, paying close attention to the story she told, about her life, about me. I, as ever, wanted to understand our life together. And as always, I was hoping to have some type of closure or breakthrough. Perhaps to finally hear her tell me without equivocating that she understood the impact of her actions.

I asked her what she thought now about how her mother, Grandma Lina, raised her.

"It's hard for me to even say 'mother,'" she said. "I don't talk about my mother except as 'her' or 'she.' I never knew love from her. I was never kissed; I was never hugged. There was no physical connection, no bond. It—it was that bad. There was never any encouragement—there was never anything from her."

"Do you remember asking for attention at all?"

"No, I withdrew. I'm a middle kid, so there was my brother for her to deal with and then there was my young sister who got all the attention. So, I became the caretaker. There was no childhood."

I nodded. "But you see how weird that is though, because you

203

weren't the caretaker for us."

"I know but think about it. If you think about the psychology: on the kibbutz it was totally different. I mean, I was a great mom. I was so happy to have children. When we came to Seattle it was like a bomb dropped. All of a sudden, I was alone with two small children. No support, no kibbutz. No family. And your father…" She looked away for a moment, and I wondered if she was thinking about the infidelity in their marriage. "He was doing whatever he was doing".

"And then as you guys were getting older," she continued, "my whole childhood got triggered and I saw myself getting impatient and angry with you kids. I was afraid of that, because my mother was such an angry, angry woman and that scared me. I was afraid of turning into her. I didn't want to hurt you or Nava."

I kept my eyes on her the whole time she was talking. I didn't want to miss a word or an expression.

"And honestly…" She paused. "I thought, I'm not a good mother—they would be better off. So that was part of it, and part of it was that it was such a hard time. We had no money and your father had moved back to New York. And I remember saying to myself there's got to be more to life than this, there's got to be some answer. I was looking and then I found out about Bhagwan. I read some of his books and it was like a light went on. Like, oh my god this is me, they're talking about me." She thought a moment. "You know, you have to be so unhappy to search—I mean, if your life is good you don't search."

I remember living with her in those days in Seattle when my father had just left for New Jersey. I felt nervous around her, unsettled. I remember how much time she'd spend in her room, how she had grown quiet and removed. It was in the blue house, the last place the three of us lived together.

"Did you have the urge to hit us?" I asked.

"I did—my temper. I could feel it. It was ready to burst. I had to, like, squash it."

It wasn't easy to hear that she was on the verge of physically or emotionally abusing us, but when I was a kid I knew something was really wrong. I felt that we weren't happy together—that she never seemed happy with me.

"I don't think it was easy for any of us," she continued. "But I did really believe you were better off with your father."

"I didn't know that you felt that way. That because you were trying to protect us you missed out."

"Of course, I missed out. I missed out on your childhood. I missed out on a lot of things." She looked down at her hands. "I have a lot of grief and—"

Her voice cracked and I almost couldn't hear her.

"—and sadness about it, I do." The word sadness was more breath than word.

"Any time we've talked about it before, you've never said it this way."

"I think you were younger, you were angry," she said, "and I don't think at times you were receptive or I was able to talk about it. I think you and I have grown closer and I feel more connected with you. I think you're more open."

"Yeah." I nodded. In all our brief attempts over the years to have this conversation, we had always fallen apart. She'd grown defensive, and I had gone on the attack. We never made it anywhere beyond this old, heavy hurt that neither of us could repair. I'm not sure what was different this time. I don't know if it was because I was older or that I listened better. I felt for the first time ever that she was really with me. That she was letting me see her.

"There is a part of me that wanted to be free," she continued. "I'd always been responsible from the time I was a kid. And I'd always taken care of everyone. But I didn't go to India to become free from you. I went for spiritual reasons. I was searching—" She cut herself off and looked at me, shaking her head in disbelief. "It sounds so naïve now. But what—I was thirty-one years old. I wanted enlightenment and I wanted to be at peace and I wanted to be happy."

"Uh huh."

"And you know I wanted to take both you and your sister."

"I think that would have been crazy. You know what happened to some of those kids."

"No, I don't know. What happened to kids?"

"Mom, there were no boundaries. They were wild. There were twelve-year-olds walking around with grown men."

"I didn't know that. Are you sure about that?"

"Not everywhere but at least on the ranch. Adults could have sex in front of their kids...there was no..."

"Really? I didn't see that though."

"But you know some people call him the Sex Guru."

"What he said was everyone should be free and you shouldn't have to be bound by marriage, and—"

"But, did any one of your friends—"

"We were never wild—"

"No, but did you ever think, Wait a minute, kids are good things. Why shouldn't we have kids?"

"He didn't say not to have kids."

"Yes, he did," I said more firmly than I'd said anything else up until this point. I knew this from my research and from interviews I'd seen in *Wild Wild Country*. "He was hoping people would get sterilized and have vasectomies."

"I don't think I knew that. I wasn't in the inner circle."

"You weren't in the one in Oregon for very long."

"No, I was in the last part of it. The last five months that it existed."

"Yeah." I realized that I had kind of jumped in and let her off the hook. I knew it was a pattern I had—to save her. Which may be why I went in again and tried to push her for more.

"But when you left me and Nava the second time when I was in middle school, we were more independent by then. Did you still feel you weren't going to be a good mom?"

"Um..." Her voice wavered a little.

"Or was it just too much?"

I saw I was getting into touchier stuff. But for some reason I wasn't afraid. Maybe it was because I sensed we were at a point in our relationship we'd never gotten to before.

"I mean, because I was twelve," I added.

"I think what happened was—that was after my mother died, right?"

I nodded once and waited. I knew she had to know when this was without asking and I grew nervous she was going to hedge. I didn't want her to run away. I needed her to level with me and to level with herself, to see her be strong enough for both of us for once. I needed her to stay.

"And I was supposed to get both of you," she went on, searching her memory for what had happened between us the very last time in my childhood I had felt hope I'd get to live with her again. Then she began to sound vague. "And I was looking for an apartment. I remember it was in Queens…and I freaked out because I couldn't afford it. And your dad said he was going to give some money but it was not going to be enough to live on."

"Yeah," I said, but I bristled. I wanted more. I wanted her to use her years and years of therapy and whatever bravery she could muster to tell the truth. Her truth, no matter how much she thought it might be the wrong answer. And I knew it was, of course, a trap. Because there are so many wrong answers in our story and very few right ones.

The right ones were to have been able to stay, to have been able to be the mother I wanted her to be, but she hadn't. So all she could do to make it better now was to be honest. But I didn't know that she could ever say it—she never had before. She'd always backed away, shut down, dodged.

"I mean," she was saying, "by then, in New York, the rents in 1985, the early 80s—"

"Well," I said, "what about staying put and seeing us on the weekends?"

I heard my husband's voice nearby; the kids were finishing their game in the other room. I knew this bubble in time I'd invited her into, this space I'd made for us, could pop any moment.

"Um," she said.

I waited.

I felt the part of me that had been disappointed in her so many times begin to prepare for that disappointment again. I felt my face begin to harden in anticipation of her excuse. I braced myself for it.

"I ran away," she said.

I froze. I could hardly believe what I heard.

"That's what I did. I ran away."

"Mom. That's the first time you've ever said it."

She nodded and went on. "You know there's that whole thing about fight, flight or freeze."

"Fight or flight?" I hadn't heard about freeze.

"Yes, fight or flight but there's also freeze. Which I do. And flight. Which I've done."

"Uh huh."

"Many times."

We both laughed a little. It wasn't funny, but it was.

She continued, "I just...run away."

I searched her face. "When do you fight?"

"I didn't. That's the problem...I think that it became too much for me. I didn't know how I was going to do it. I didn't know how I was going to support us. I was afraid. And what did I do? I ran."

She widened her eyes and with mock enthusiasm, making fun of her former self. "Oh, an ashram? Sure! Why not? But," she said, shaking her head, "it makes no sense to me now. I mean, I would never do that now. Not even in the last twenty years would I have done something like that, but back then..."

"Right. But you're also not needed now the way you were needed twenty or thirty years ago."

"No, I mean the person I am, the person who I've become, wouldn't have done that."

"Right. But it's bad timing. Because you've had more stable addresses now than in my entire childhood and back then we wanted you to stay in one place."

"I think part of it was..." She paused, took a breath. "I think I didn't feel needed. I didn't feel my worth. I didn't have that sense I was important."

I know that's always been true of her, and I blame Grandma Lina for knocking the strength out of her. For taking away her sense of self.

We were on a roll and nobody had interrupted us yet, so I went on. "It's funny, because you've said that I'm a strong person and I was resilient. Through the years you've said to me, 'You were so independent, I didn't think you needed me.' I worry because I feel like it's putting the blame on me a little for not being a softer, more vulnerable kid."

"No! I mean, you weren't but that was fine. I mean it was—"

"But I want you to know that when you say I was independent or you didn't feel needed, I feel like you're saying I was capable of handling you leaving."

"Remember, you were very strong."

"That's not the point—"

"But," she said, "*I* wasn't strong."

"Mom," I said, "you want your mom to stay no matter how old you are."

"Right. Right."

I let out the breath I hadn't realized I'd been holding. "For so long I've felt that because of who I am, you thought it was okay to go."

"That's who you are, and that's who you were as a kid, but that isn't why I left."

"But is it part of the reason why you rationalized it was okay?"

"No, I thought your father would be a better parent."

"You know," I said, thinking about how he'd gone to New Jersey to live with Tracy and her girls when I was five, "it's not lost on me that he left us first."

She nodded. I nodded. Like two old ladies on a porch stoop.

"What was his plan, do you think?" I asked. "Had you not dumped us with him in New Jersey, when was he planning on seeing us?"

"I don't know. He never said. And you know that was a terrible, terrible time."

"I felt it."

"It was just awful."

"Do you think he was trying to punish you by cutting and running? Like, *You want to get a divorce? Okay, I'm out.*"

"Well, you know the thing he said to me, about Tracy and her girls in Newark—he said the most important thing for him was to be a father and have a wife, or maybe it was to have a family and be a father. That's why he went with Tracy. But what about you guys?"

"Yeah."

"So he left. And we were dirt poor. We had nothing. Those years were horrible; no resources, no family…I mean, I made do. I worked. But think about it; eight years on a kibbutz and then dropped into city living. And being a single parent. And it was a hard transition for you. I don't know about Nava because she was young."

"I don't know that she remembers it much."

"I don't think she does. But for you, to fit in with these kids, and a whole new world for you. I mean *that* was hard."

"Yeah. I didn't get it. I couldn't figure Seattle out."

"You were a sabra. These were not our people."

We sat together shaking our heads, remembering, and she said, "It was so hard. So hard."

"Would you say that was the worst time? After your childhood, the worst?"

"Yes, the worst. The worst period of my life." I heard her breath tremble when she exhaled.

I reached over to hold her hands. Tears ran down her face.

"Mom—"

She exhaled a jagged breath. Wiped her eye. "Not an easy time."

"Are you thinking about when you were married to Dad? I know your childhood was also hard…"

"Well, you know I went into—what is it? The fire into the frying pan?"

"The frying pan into the fire." Both of us are terrible at idioms but I can usually fix hers.

"Right, I went from the frying pan into the fire. I married someone who was very domineering like my mother."

"Nobody gets away free in this family."

"Yeah," she said wiping her cheeks with the back of her hands.

"Mom," I said while we were still alone, "thank you."

Just then I heard my fourteen-year-old daughter call at the top of her lungs like she always does when she's looking for me. "Mom?!" She and her brother were approaching from the other room.

"In the living room, honey!" I called back just as loudly. "With Grandma."

And just like that the spell was broken.

~

I understand how we live now can't change the things that happened to our family then, and I would never go back to my childhood. I've spent my whole life, except for the first six years of it, pining after my mother and the relationship we didn't get to have. It's an old wound that won't ever completely heal, but it finally hurts less.

My mother doesn't have to keep paying for who she was so long ago, and I don't have to punish her or keep a part of myself away in order to love her.

This is our relationship. This is what we have. We can be safe together.

Glossary

Ashram—A secluded building, often the residence of a guru, used for religious retreat or instruction.

Bat Mitzvah—A Jewish coming of age ritual for girls. Bar Mitzvah is the coming of age ritual for boys.

Beit Tinokot—Literally "house for children" or children's house where kibbutz babies and kids lived and slept.

Bimah—The raised platform in the synagogue from which the Torah is read and services led.

Bindi—A bindi is a colored dot worn on the center of the forehead, originally by Hindus and Jains from the Indian subcontinent.

Challah—Challah is a special bread in Jewish cuisine, usually braided and typically eaten on ceremonial occasions such as Shabbat and major Jewish holidays.

Darshan—A divine blessing often bestowed by a guru to his follower.

Est—Erhard Seminars Training organization founded by Werner Erhard aka John Paul Rosenberg in 1971 that offered a two-weekend 60-hour seminar aimed at personal transformation. Est seminars took place from late 1971 to late 1984.

Kibbutz—A collective farm or settlement in modern Israel based on a high level of social and economical sharing, equality, direct demo-cracy, tight social relations including collective rearing of children. Modern industries have taken over a significant role in the Kibbutz economy, and the level of sharing has dropped significantly.

Kibbutznik—Someone who lives on a kibbutz.

Klutz—Yiddish, a clumsy or stupid person; a dolt.

Mazel Tov—A Jewish phrase used to express congratulations for a happy and significant occasion or event.

Purim—A Jewish holiday which commemorates the saving of the Jewish people from Haman, an Achaemenid Persian Empire official who was planning to kill all the Jews, as recounted in the Book of Esther.

Ranjneeshees—Followers of Bhagwan Shree Rajneesh.

Rajneeshpuram—A Religious intentional community in Wasco County, Oregon, briefly incorporated as a city between 1981 and 1988 whose population consisted entirely of Rajneeshees.

Rancho Rajneesh—The 100-square-mile ranch in central Oregon that became Bhagwan's Oregon commune.

Rugelach—A small, filled pastry originating in the Jewish communities of Poland.

Sabra—A native-born Israeli and the cactus fruit that has a prickly exterior and a soft interior.

Sannyasin—A Sanskrit word that describes someone who has reached the life stage of sannyasa, or "renouncement of material possession", who lives only to perfect their understanding of the spiritual world.

Sari—A garment of southern Asian women that consists of several yards of lightweight cloth draped so that one end forms a skirt and the other a head or shoulder covering.

Schtick—A Yiddish word meaning comic theme or gimmick.

Shabbat—Hebrew, the day of rest from sunset Friday night to Saturday night and the centerpiece of Jewish life.

Torah—The first five books of the 24 books of the Hebrew Bible.

Acknowledgments

I could not have written this book without the support of my family. Their patience, understanding, and insight enabled me to keep looking at our history from fresh angles. I'm humbled by and grateful for their willingness to revisit difficult memories and for their love.

I'm also grateful to the teachers with whom I was privileged to study early on, especially University of Washington faculty Larry Cheek and Scott Driscoll, Anna Balint and Cara Diacanoff at Hugo House, and Marie-Helene Bertino at the One Story Summer Writers Conference. I'm indebted to the workshop groups I've been part of over the years who guided me with their honesty and encouragement and helped shape my voice and my belief in myself. Thank you to my dear friend Lauren Eckstein for taking a chance and giving me my first real writing assignment way back at SUNY B.

Thank you to my friends and roommates and the faculty at Pacific University's Master of Fine Arts program, especially Sanjiv Battacharya, Judy Blunt, Jack Driscoll, Craig Lesley, Mike Magnuson, and Jennifer Scanlon. Special thanks to my generous advisors Pete Fromm, Scott Korb, and the memoirist I aspire to be, Debra Gwartney, who read this story when I thought it was an essay and encouraged me to *just write the memoir already.*

To Jason Allen, Wendy Colbert, Susan DeFreitas, Mike Magnuson, Jennifer Munro, and the indefatigable Jessica Lipnack, thank you for taking this manuscript on and editing it through its different stages.

And to my dear Seattle friends, especially Alice, Birgit, Leslie, Meg, Missy, and Rachel who check in to see how the writing is going and have always been patient when I give them the long answer, thank you for your support, the snacks, and for rooting me on.

Thank you to my publisher Diane Windsor for your belief in this project and in me. I am so happy to bring this into the world under your steady hand.

And, to my husband, my daughter, and my son, I love you with everything I have. You are the life I dreamed of.

About the Author

Ronit Plank is a writer, teacher, and podcaster with work in *The Atlantic, The Washington Post, The Rumpus, The Iowa Review,* and *American Literary Review,* among others. She is host and producer of the award-winning podcast *And Then Everything Changed,* featuring interviews with survivors, authors, thought leaders, and people in recovery about pivotal moments in their lives and decisions that have defined them.

She has an MFA in Non-Fiction from Pacific University, and *When She Comes Back* is her first book. Her short story collection, *Home Is A Made-Up Place,* won Hidden River Arts' 2020 Eludia Award and will be published in 2022.

For more about her work visit https://ronitplank.com/